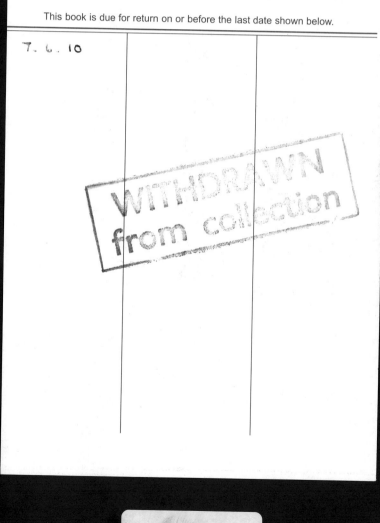

Moulton College

NORTHAMPTONSHIRE

4-H GUIDE
TO RAISING CHICKENS

Tara Kindschi

Voyageur Press

A portion of the sales of this product will be used to promote 4-H educational programs. No endorsement of this product by 4-H is implied or intended. Use of the 4-H Name & Emblem is authorized by USDA.

4-H is a community of six million young people across America learning leadership, citizenship, and life skills. National 4-H Council is the private sector, non-profit partner of National 4-H Headquarters (USDA). The 4-H programs are implemented by the 106 Land-Grant Universities and the Cooperative Extension System through their 3,100 local Extension offices across the country. Learn more about 4-H at www.4-H.org. 18 USC 707

First published in 2009 by Voyageur Press, an imprint of MBI Publishing Company, 400 First Avenue North, Suite 300, Minneapolis, MN 55401 USA

Copyright © 2009 by Tara Kindschi

Voyageur Press titles are also available at discounts in bulk quantity for industrial or sales-promotional use. For details write to Special Sales Manager at MBI Publishing Company, 400 First Avenue North, Suite 300, Minneapolis, MN 55401 USA.

To find out more about our books, visit us online at www.voyageurpress.com.

Library of Congress Cataloging-in-Publication Data

Kindschi, Tara, 1970-
4-H guide to raising chickens / Tara Kindschi.—1st ed.
        p. cm.
Includes index.
ISBN 978-0-7603-3628-1 (flexibound)
1. Chickens. I. Title.
SF487.K5618 2010
636.5—dc22

                                                        2009015300

Editor by Amy Glaser
Design Manager: Katie Sonmor
Designed by Pauline Molinari
Cover designed by the Book Designers
Front cover main photo: © Gary John Norman/Getty Images
Front cover 3rd inset photo: © Eileen Hart/iStockphoto
Back cover 1st photo: © Jaren Jai Wicklund/Shutterstock

Book reviewed by:
Dr. Laura Perry Johnson
Program Development Coordinator
University of Georgia

Printed in China

CONTENTS

GETTING STARTED WITH CHICKENS

Welcome to the world of raising chickens! Chickens, like all other domestic animals, have unique personalities that make keeping them a rewarding animal project and life experience. Unlike larger animals, chickens can be raised in a limited space and on a small budget. They are a great size for a youth project, and the rewards are bountiful in many ways.

Chickens have unique personalities and habits that a young flock owner can enjoy. Also, their size does not intimidate small children. The responsibility required to care for chickens through daily chores and record-keeping can create a good learning experience. *Kris Even*

A Bit of History

Many people have played important roles in defining and developing the poultry hobby to make it what it is today. Do you ever wonder where all the different breeds of chickens come from, or how showing poultry got started and who defined the rules?

Domesticated fowl have been in North America since the *Mayflower* landed at Plymouth Rock in 1620. Interest in poultry grew along with the New World population. Imported stock played a significant role in the popularity of chickens. Brahmas, Cochins, and Langshans were imported from China and the East Indies in the early 1800s. The Leghorn was first imported in the 1840s. This stock was further developed into the different varieties we see today. All of the American chicken breeds were developed in North America using stock from varied sources, hence the names Plymouth Rock, Rhode Island, and Delaware.

The first known poultry exhibition in America was held in Massachusetts during 1849. Over one thousand birds were exhibited by 219 exhibitors and drew a crowd of ten thousand spectators. Many shows followed, and some of today's clubs have hosted a show for over one hundred years.

The American Poultry Association (APA) was organized in 1873, primarily to standardize the many fowl varieties found in North America. In doing so, the *Standard of Excellence* was printed and contained descriptions of forty-one large fowl and twenty bantam varieties. By 1905 the book was called the *American Standard of Perfection* and contained eighty-six drawings alongside the descriptions. The *American Standard of Perfection* has undergone many revisions and printings. It is now available in a black-and-white or a full-color version with descriptions of all the recognized breeds and illustrations of many varieties.

A single-comb, light-brown Leghorn hen shows the complex color pattern of her variety. This Leghorn variety was admitted to the *American Standard of Perfection* in 1874. The white earlobe and yellow legs indicate she is a Leghorn. Hens of this breed are prolific layers of large white eggs. *Shelly Sonsalla*

This pair of Wyandotte bantams exhibits a lovely blue color and good feather condition. Note the male's natural tendency to be in front of the female, which shows his territorial, protective instinct. This is his way of showing that he considers himself owner of the hen or hens and will protect them from you or other roosters. *Corallina Breuer*

The popularity of breeds and varieties of birds being used for flocks has varied throughout the years. When almost every family had a flock for home consumption and table use, a dual-purpose breed that tolerated mixed climates was preferred. As farming practices changed and more people lived in urban areas, more specialized breeds came to the forefront. Some farmers raised strictly meat birds, while other farms diversified with efficient egg-layer houses. Today's trend for locally grown, wholesome food has sparked a resurgence in backyard poultry keeping and raising heritage breeds.

The poultry show world, also known as the "fancy," has witnessed many trends with regard to chicken breeds that are shown. Imported stock was in demand when unusual varieties were shown. Breeders who developed the varieties found in the American class spent countless time and resources getting their breeds admitted into the *American Standard of Perfection*. Bantams and their unique traits have been mainstays of the fancy. Today, it is common for bantam breed entries to account for more than double the number of large fowl entries. The bantams' smaller size for keeping and transporting is a deciding factor for many enthusiasts.

Poultry As a 4-H Project

Poultry and 4-H make a great combination. The 4-H poultry program offers many youth activities and classes, including information about poultry production of all types, how to judge poultry and poultry products, and preparing foods using poultry products, as well as public presentations that utilize information learned while participating in the poultry program. Competitions are held at the county, district, state, and national levels with rewards that include an increased appreciation of the poultry industry's impact on our lives and recognition in the form of awards, prizes, trips, and collegiate scholarships.

Poultry Friends

Whether it is with a breeder who sells you your first trio of your favorite breed or a fellow 4-Her who learns the basics of bird keeping and showmanship with you, you will form many lasting friendships within the poultry hobby. You share a common interest in chickens—whether they are big Brahmas or tiny Old English Games—and talking about your experiences (both good and bad) will lead to many enjoyable conversations. In the process you will learn more firsthand tips and tricks in caring for and showing your birds, plus some life lessons along the way.

Washing your bird is a big part of getting it ready for a show. A bath removes dirt and manure from feathers. Special attention should be paid to the legs, vent, and face areas. It is a good way to spend extra time with individual birds and makes them calmer and more manageable. *DeAnn Richards*

Friendships formed by young people with a common interest in the poultry hobby can last a lifetime. Friends can share information, test each other's poultry knowledge, extend their friendship to other aspects of their lives, and more! *Patti Delaney-Ruhland*

Parts of a Chicken

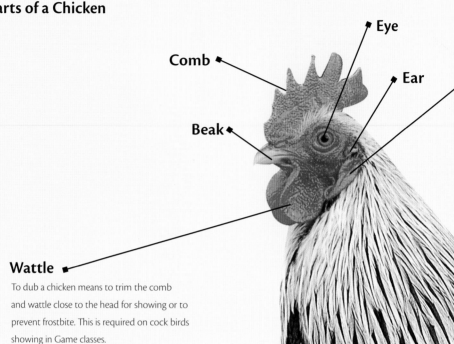

Eye

Comb

Ear

Beak

Wattle

To dub a chicken means to trim the comb and wattle close to the head for showing or to prevent frostbite. This is required on cock birds showing in Game classes.

Breast

Cornish hens are known for their huge breasts and heavy bodies. Most modern-day broiler crosses are a result of mating Cornish chickens to Plymouth Rock chickens for extremely fast growth and weight gain.

Earlobe

Check a chicken's earlobe to determine her egg color. If a hen has a whitish blue earlobe, she will always lay a pure white egg. One with a red earlobe will lay a colored egg. She will usually produce brown but could also produce shades of blue or green. A hen will lay the same color of egg her entire life because genetics, not environment, determine eggshell color.

Back

Saddle feathers

For an easy method to identify a bird's sex that works for over 95 percent of chicken breeds and crossbreeds, take a close look at the end of a feather from the hackle or saddle area. If it is pointed and shaped like an arrow, you have a male. Females have a curved, spoon-shaped end. A few breeds are classified as hen-feathered, however, which means both sexes have the curved feather of a female.

Wing

Hook

Shank

The shank is the part of a chicken's leg between the claw and the first joint. Chicken breeds with feathers growing on their shanks and sometimes on their toes are known as feather-leg breeds.

Chicken swaps feature more than just buying and selling birds. Many people will also be selling new and used cages, extra fencing, feeders, and other items. Remember to use good sanitation practices when buying used equipment for your flock, since parasites and diseases can easily be spread through this type of contact. *Tara Kindschi*

Investment Budget

Raising poultry is one of the more economical animal projects. Here is a simple breakdown of expected costs for a twelve-bird, large fowl flock if you were to purchase all new equipment and housing.

These costs can be lowered considerably if you build or reuse existing equipment or housing. Adding a fenced yard or run will increase your coop cost. Raising chicks versus buying young adults may also be more cost effective.

Start-up Expenses

5-gallon metal waterer	$25
36-inch metal trough feeder	$12
6-hole nesting box	$118
Purchased wooden coop	$1,500
Purchased pullets (12 x $8)	$96
Total estimated cost	$1,751

This old building is being converted to house chickens. A treated base and floor and a sturdy door will be added. A broad-spectrum disinfectant and a dry fogger system to disperse the disinfectant will help make sure the old wood is free of disease and parasites. *Kelly Damaschke*

This is the same building after it has been completely refurbished. The small header window allows only a limited amount of sunlight, so a light on a timer is a necessity for this converted space that is otherwise just right for a small flock of bantams. *Kelly Damaschke*

Maintenance Expenses

Based on current feed prices and pre-formulated feed at $15 per fifty-pound bag, it costs just under $45 to raise one large fowl hen for 365 days. The base feed cost for a backyard flock of twelve chickens is $540 per year.

Typical Expenses

Oyster shell (one-year supply)	$18.00
Grit (one-year supply)	$11.00
Shavings (one-year supply)	$91.00
Yearly feed bill	$540.00 ($1.48 per day)

Another cost to consider may be increased electricity. Using straw or recycled paper is a lower-cost option for bedding if they are available in your area.

Income

You also have to consider the amount of potential income you'll receive from your flock. You can expect twelve year-old laying hens to produce 8 eggs per day for a total of 4 1/2 dozen eggs per week at a value of $2.50 to $3.00 per dozen for premium eggs, all for a yearly egg value of $585.00.

The value of spent birds as meat to the family is hard to measure, but processing costs must be considered. The ethnic market value is $3.00 to $5.00 per bird.

When a budget like this is set up, there is no cost benefit associated with the experience of raising and caring for the chickens or the quality of fresh eggs and compost materials they provide. These factors must be considered above and beyond the budget sheet.

Great-tasting, beautiful eggs are the number one reason people have backyard flocks. The superior freshness and taste of these eggs can't be matched by common store-bought eggs that may be several weeks old when purchased. If you are going to sell extra eggs, you can plan to charge a premium price for your hen's bounty! *Tara Kindschi*

Frequently Asked Questions

You may have some basic questions before starting a poultry project. The following information provides quick answers that will help you get started and learn more about raising chickens.

Chickens can be more than livestock to you and your family. Their unique personalities allow them to become pets. This young man and his black Australorp pullet are having fun while getting ready for a show. *DeAnn Richards*

Breeds

How do I select a breed? Start by thinking about the color of eggs you'd like, such as brown, white, or green. What size of eggs do you prefer? Would you like a small bird to hold or a large bird that lays jumbo eggs? The standard reference for every breed and variety of purebred fowl is the *American Standard of Perfection.* This comprehensive guide may be checked out from your local library or purchased from the American Poultry

Association. Consider the economic qualities for each breed and the color of the bird. When showing chickens, a solid-color variety is easier to perfect than a patterned bird. Size and temperament are also considerations. In large fowl, the large, heavier breeds tend to be calmer than the gamey, racy-looking ones. With bantam breeds, the game breeds tend to be quick and fast. Breeds with special features may require specialized care.

What type of chicken is best for a small flock? Hens in many breeds coexist well together to allow you to have a diverse group of colors and temperaments.

What type of chicken lays the most eggs? Leghorns and egg-laying hybrid crosses will lay more eggs.

Can I mix old birds and new birds in the same flock? Yes, after the young stock is fully feathered and at about three-quarters of adult size, you can combine age groups in your flock.

There is a myth that says all white chickens lay white eggs. This is not true. The color of the female's ear lobe will tell you if she will lay a white or colored egg. A red ear lobe means a colored egg, and a white ear lobe means she will lay a white egg. This rose-comb Rhode Island White chick will lay brown eggs. *Kendall Babcock*

The size of a chicken can be extreme! This showy black Cochin cockerel dominates in overall size and mass over the smaller buff Brahma cockerel. These two breeds would not do well sharing a coop. They can still be part of a small home flock when given enough room to free-range and go their separate ways when they are locked in the coop at night. *Kendall Babcock*

Can I mix breeds in one coop? Yes, several breeds can be housed in one coop with a few key considerations. Within the chicken world, there are regular-sized chickens called large fowl and miniature chickens called bantams. It is best to stick with one size for your flock.

General Care

Do chickens require daily care? Yes, chickens require daily observation, egg collection, feeding, and watering.

What are the basic requirements for food, water, and shelter? Fresh, clean water must be available twenty-four hours a day. A complete ration of feed should be designed for your birds' age and offered as free-choice or in multiple feedings. If feed runs out during the day, add more feeder space. Grit and oyster shell are two dietary add-ons that all laying hens need. Housing, even during nice weather, is as much for security from predators as it is for shelter. A dry, draft-free shelter is required for protection on cold or wet days.

Collecting eggs is a fun aspect of daily chores. Keep a chart of how many eggs are laid per day. Calculating your feed costs for those eggs is a good way to learn basic economics. *Kelly Damaschke*

Keeping a laying flock is a year-round project. Chickens are quite hardy if they are healthy and given enough food and protection from dampness and drafts. The addition of a light and heat lamp keeps this small flock cozy in this windowless converted coop on even the worst winter days. *Kelly Damaschke*

Backyard flocks enjoy being outside even when snow is on the ground. Here a mixed flock of hens follows the shoveled snow paths around the yard. Chickens will stay indoors during storms and extreme windy days, but the fresh air and sunlight feel good to them, even in colder temperatures. *Shelly Sonsalla*

What is the ideal flock size for someone starting out? You should begin your flock with twelve adults, if your space allows. Start with twenty-five straight-run chicks in three to four breeds, watch them grow, keep your favorite male, market the extra other males, and have eleven hens. They will produce enough for a family of four plus extras for family and friends.

How do I care for my chickens when it's cold outside? A heated water base keeps the drinking water from freezing; a light combats the darkness of winter; deep, dry bedding provides comfort; and a draft-free shelter helps prevent frostbite.

How will my chicks arrive from a hatchery? You can pick them up from a hatchery, or they will be shipped via the U.S. Postal Service and can be picked up from your local post office.

Where do I keep chicks when they arrive from a hatchery? Place them in a brooder (heated area for starting chicks) or

container placed in a warm, dry location away from predators, including cats. A basement or spare bathroom in a house or a heated garage or shed can be used if the outside temperatures are below fifty degrees.

Standard chick shipping boxes are used by most hatcheries. This box is suitable for one hundred large fowl chicks, with twenty-five per compartment. This is the number of chicks needed to keep the space warm enough for them to survive one to three days in shipping. *Tara Kindschi*

How much space do I need to figure per bird? Allow a minimum of 1.5 to 2.5 square feet per bird for bantams and 2 to 3 square feet per bird for large fowl.

How easy is it to build my own coop? Building a coop from scratch or modifying an existing building is relatively easy. Follow the square footage requirements for the number of chickens you will have. Also include room for all the following: areas to eat and drink; nesting boxes for laying hens; roosts for sleeping at night; windows or light sources; ventilation in the form of windows, fans, or vents; and a solid floor for easy cleaning and predator protection.

Where do I obtain plans? Your county agricultural extension agent has access to many types of coop plans. Copying a friend's coop design may also work. Some farm supply stores offer ready-made kits.

How do I move chickens? Use one hand to grip and hold the legs and the other hand to keep the wings from flapping. Hold the bird close to your body to keep the bird stable.

How do I make my coop predator-proof? Have a tight floor and roof and make sure strong wire covers any opening, including vents.

What are good roost designs? The roost should include several heights for different breeds, with each row set back from the previous row to keep droppings from falling on other birds. Rounded wood dowels are best for the birds to grip.

Can chickens sleep and lay eggs in the same place? In a caged setup, hens have no choice and will lay their eggs wherever they can. In a coop situation, keeping birds from sleeping in the nest boxes is advisable because their droppings make the area dirty. Anytime you find a bird sleeping in a nest box, move her to a roost.

The diversity of breeds may tempt you to buy too many birds. Limit your purchases to correspond with the space you have. Overcrowding birds, whether they are chicks or adults, can lead to cannibalism and disease outbreaks because the birds are more stressed. Culling excess roosters and nonproductive females from your flock will also help keep your coop from being too crowded. *Corallina Breuer*

What do I use for bedding? Absorbency is the key when looking for bedding. Wood shavings are the most useful but are more expensive than using straw. Shredded paper and sawdust are also options.

How often do I need to clean out the coop? Where do I put the manure? Your coop needs to be cleaned whenever the bedding gets damp or soiled enough to form a ball. This may mean removing and freshening bedding around the waterer and under the roost every week or two. If the house doesn't have enough ventilation and the bedding becomes damp, improve the ventilation, clean the entire coop, and replace the bedding.

The dirty bedding and droppings are too high in nitrogen to put directly on a garden. It is better to compost them to an unused area of the yard, turn it regularly, and use the compost next season as fertilizer and mulch. If you are using the deep-litter method, you can remove the old layer and use it directly where you want it, since you basically did the composting in the coop.

Do chickens need extra light in winter? A few hours of light a day will give birds time to feed and drink, but they tend to sleep from dusk to dawn. Provide twelve to sixteen hours of light for maximum egg production. You can provide them with less light if you aren't concerned about getting eggs and don't mind a long winter break.

What keeps chickens "entertained" while cooped up so they don't fight or peck at one another? They like to scratch in the loose bedding for hours. Sprinkling their treats in the bedding will keep them busy during long winter days when they don't care to be outside.

How much will it cost to feed a chicken per week? A fifty-pound bag of layer feed ranges from nine dollars to eighteen dollars per bag and will feed one hen for 125 days. Laying hens need an average of about one-half pound of feed per day. (Consider 50 percent are laying.) That computes to eight to fifteen cents per day. Figure on more or less depending on weather conditions, amount of scratch feed, and foraging by the birds.

Do you feed chickens for meat different than those raised for eggs? Yes, a different premix feed is needed for meat chickens and should only be offered for sixteen hours a day, versus free-choice feed for egg-layers.

These fast-growing Cornish-cross chicks are shown in a manufactured brooder. Birds of this breed need to be raised separately from those of other breeds due to their extreme growth and feed intake requirements. For a poultry enthusiast, they are a nice addition to a fair's market class offerings. *Corallina Breuer*

Can meat and egg chickens be raised together in the same coop? No, the diet and habits of meat chickens and egg-laying chickens are too different.

Where do I buy feed? Feed can be purchased at pet stores, garden centers, hardware stores, and feed mills.

Can I raise the grain for my chickens? Yes, but grain that you raise should be used as a treat rather than a substitute for a purchased balanced blend.

Can I buy corn and oats directly from a farmer? Yes, but corn purchased directly should be ground with minerals to make a complete ration. Local feed mills have a recipe to follow. Such purchases are often too large a quantity for home flock use, however.

What is "pastured" poultry? For "pastured" poultry, the birds are confined in a caged area of one to three square feet per bird on lush pasture that is moved once or twice daily. Both meat and egg-laying chickens can be raised using this method.

Can chickens live only on grass? For a short time, yes, chickens can live on grass, but they do require many nutrients not found in all climates and types of grass, therefore grains

and minerals should be included in their diet.

Can I feed extra produce from my garden or table scraps to my chickens? Yes, table scraps and produce are fine as long as the fruits or vegetables are overripe but not rotten and don't smell foul. Avoid meat scraps.

Can eggshells be composted? Yes, composting the shells is better than giving them back to the birds, since this can lead to an egg-eating habit.

What facilities do I need for larger-scale production? To begin a large-scale production, you will need a specially designed laying hen house that can fit over five thousand layers, the starting size for egg production flocks in the United States. Broiler houses typically need to be twice that size to be economically feasible. Niche markets, such as organic meat birds, can have smaller flock sizes.

Showing

Where are chicken shows held? County fairs, school fairs, and American Poultry Association (APA)–sanctioned shows are often hosted by local clubs that rent fairground space.

Proudly showing off your poultry project at the fair is a goal of many young people and is easily accomplished, since chickens are quite economical to buy, raise, and transport. Here a still-growing patridge Cochin and his excited owner settle into the fair. *Patti Delaney-Ruhland*

A young golden Sebright pullet enjoys the companionship of her bantam flockmates. Although she has another set of feathers to grow before adulthood, she appears to have too dark of a lacing pattern to be good show quality. *Shelly Sonsalla*

What age do you need to be to show chickens? The 4-H Junior show starts in third grade. Some county fairs have open shows for any age, and APA Junior shows are for anyone through age nineteen.

How old do the chickens have to be before they can be shown? To do well, chickens should have their final adult plumage. Over four months of age is a general rule, although some large, slow-growing breeds need more time to mature.

What type of chicken is best for a 4-H or FFA project? A purebred in a breed that you like for showing would be best. A Cornish cross is ideal for a meat project.

Marketing

Can raising chickens be a small business for me? Yes. Meat production, egg-laying, or livestock sales are all possibilities. Do your homework first. Make an income and expense sheet and factor in all of the following costs: birds, feed, electricity, supplies like feeders and fencing, 10 percent rearing loss, and processing costs. Food safety regulations for selling meat and eggs can be very complex and costly, so do your research thoroughly before you start. Your local county extension agent can provide you with the information to help you with your planning process.

Are eggs good for you? Yes, they are a good source of protein and essential vitamins and minerals.

Are brown eggs better than white eggs? No. However, eggs from chickens fed a rich and varied diet may have a richer yellow yolk color. The improved taste in eggs from a small flock is often due to the freshness of the eggs.

How do I market eggs? Word of mouth is best for marketing small quantities through family, neighbors, farmers, and farmers' markets. Check with your state agriculture department to see what licensing may be required if you sell directly to the public versus off the farm.

How do I promote eggs? Offer a free dozen to anyone who expresses an interest in your birds. The freshness and rich yolk color will have them paying a premium price for the next dozen.

How much space do I need to store eggs? A shelf in your refrigerator will hold six to eight dozen eggs.

What happens to eggs in hot or cold weather? Eggs remain freshest when stored at a temperature of forty to fifty degrees. Colder temperatures can lead to freezing and shell breakage. Warmer temperatures cause the nutrients to break down faster. A refrigerated egg will store safely for over three weeks.

Can I freeze extra eggs? Yes. Remove the egg from the shell and put the white and yolk into a sealable container. A small glass jar works well. Eggs store well for up to one month or sometimes more and are best used for cooking rather than frying.

Can I butcher chickens myself? What do I need to know? Yes, you can butcher chickens. However, you may be limited in selling the meat due to state food safety regulations. Cleanliness is rule number one. You can find a complete guide to butchering chickens in a homestead magazine or from your county agricultural extension agent.

How can I market meat? Selling through word of mouth or at a farmers' market is a good way to start.

Are there any rules and regulations for marketing the meat? Be sure to check your state's food safety and licensing rules and regulations before selling any meat. Some states require that you only sell from home if birds are butchered at home or in a state-licensed facility. Depending on the quantity of birds sold, you may need to process your birds at federally inspected facilities if you want to sell them elsewhere. Transporting processed birds generally requires licensing.

Can I do anything with the feathers? Fly-tying is a hobby that uses the hackle feathers of males in fishing lures.

Health

What precautions do I take when introducing new birds to my flock? Use a quarantine method that involves keeping new birds in a separate area for thirty days while they acclimate to your feed and conditions. Also watch for signs of disease or parasites during this time.

How do I tell if my chickens are healthy? Daily observation is important. Look for subtle clues, such as behavior—low feed and water consumption, huddled birds—or wheezy breathing and runny droppings. These are signs of a disease or a health problem.

What if one chicken dies? Will the others get sick? Do others need to be tested or checked? If so, how and when? Loss of one bird should not be cause for alarm if the rest appear healthy. Chickens can have heart attacks, cancer, and a number of other illnesses that are not contagious and go unnoticed to even a close observer. If you lose two birds in a day, immediately stop and look for clues. Take notes of any changes in habits and feed intake. Separate any birds that appear unhealthy. Read over the disease list in this guide, narrow it down, and if you are unsure, consult a veterinarian, poultry expert, or county agricultural extension agent.

What do I do when a chicken dies? Remove the body from your other birds as soon as possible. Check for signs of disease. Don't dispose of (bury or cremate) the body until you are sure it did not die of a disease. The body may be needed for testing if you have a serious disease outbreak. How old was the bird? If over three years of age, it could be a heart attack or other age-related illness. Did a predator kill the bird? If so, be sure to check that your coop is secure.

What is a "reportable" disease? Any infectious disease that your state deems relevant as an animal health concern is considered a "reportable" disease. Check with your state veterinarian or county agricultural extension agent to get a current list and learn about reportable diseases.

What is bird flu? Will I catch it if my chickens get it? Avian Influenza, also known as bird flu, is not currently found in the U.S. and is not listed in this guide's disease section. States are doing voluntary testing of some flocks for observation only. This form of influenza can make humans sick and may lead to death.

Will chicken parasites transfer to me? No, unlike human head lice, the parasites don't feed or survive on human skin.

Special Considerations

Do all chickens get along? Males of any breed are naturally territorial, and it is best to have only one male for a small flock or keep extra males in separate pens to eliminate fighting. Hens will work out a "pecking order" for flock status when first introduced, but once that is set, hens are sociable creatures.

What does "hen-pecked" mean? It is part of the social order within a flock in which the top hen tends to peck at all the lower ones to show her dominance.

How can I introduce new chickens to the flock? Several methods work well for introducing hens into a flock. Moving new chickens into the coop after dark will help integrate those birds into the flock. Allow space and cover for a younger, smaller, or slower male when adding another rooster to avoid serious damage from any fighting.

Are chickens considered to be livestock or pets? Chickens fit into either category. They all have unique personalities and will recognize humans and schedules. Unlike a pet, they do have economic qualities in the form of egg and meat production.

Fast Facts

How much care do chickens require? Daily feeding and watering, egg collection twice a day, and weekly cleaning chores.

How long do chickens live? Chickens can live twelve years or more. A hen's most productive egg-laying time is nine months to two years of age.

At what age do chickens start laying eggs? Only hens lay eggs, and they start laying around six months of age and keep laying except for molting breaks.

What is molting? Molting is the shedding of old feathers so new ones can grow. This happens every year with adult chickens. Hens will stop laying during molt and begin laying again when new feathers have grown in.

How many years do hens lay eggs? Ideally hens lay eggs throughout their lives, with the highest production at one year of age and dropping off every year thereafter. Older hens (over three years) may lay in short seasonal bursts and often produce one larger, jumbo-sized egg.

Do my chickens need to have access to the outdoors? No, but they do love to get out on nice days. Foraging (looking for their own food) is something chickens enjoy.

How can I keep my chickens laying eggs year-round? Provide comfortable quarters with plenty of space, dry bedding, no drafts, and extra lighting. Provide twelve to sixteen hours of combined sunlight and artificial lighting each day as needed.

How many eggs per day do chickens lay? The maximum number of eggs a chicken can lay in a day is one. A great laying hen may lay three hundred eggs in a year. She will take a break to molt and have a few off days.

Do I need to have a rooster in the flock?
Hens lay eggs whether you have a rooster or not. A rooster tends to be colorful; the crow is fun to hear if you aren't disturbing close neighbors, and he is a natural leader of the flock. You will need a rooster to fertilize eggs if you wish to hatch any chicks.

How many roosters can I have with my hens? One for every twelve to twenty-four hens is enough for fertility reasons. Too many roosters can cause fighting among the males, and the hens can be mated too often, which causes feather breakage and loss.

Are some breeds of roosters more aggressive than others? To an extent, all roosters will show aggression toward other roosters. Game and fighting breeds are obviously very aggressive, even toward humans. Cochins and Brahmas are generally mellow.

How long does it take to raise a chicken for meat? A broiler meat cross takes six to twelve weeks, depending on the size of carcass you want. An excess purebred rooster needs to grow for six to eight months.

Who will like my chickens aside from me? The whole family will love the eggs. Any neighbors or family members with gardens appreciate the chickens eating their garden scraps, as well as the compost from the coop.

Can chickens roam freely? Yes, although predators are a problem, and the chickens may get into the garden or flowerbeds and cause damage by eating produce or scratching. Chickens also don't know to stay off roads or the neighbors' lawns.

Started birds are sometimes offered for sale at shows and swaps. A lot of the cost of raising these birds, such as electricity and starter feed, has already been invested. You can usually determine the sex of these birds by looking for sex feathers. Plan to pay almost twice as much for started birds than for day-old chicks of the same breed. It is very important to follow quarantine procedures when you take purchased birds home. *Tara Kindschi*

Why do chickens scratch the ground?
They are looking for bugs and hidden seeds.

Should my chickens have access to dirt?
It's not mandatory, but they do like to scratch and take dust baths.

Will they find their way back into the coop at night? Once the birds are acclimated to a coop, they will naturally "go home" at dusk.

Can chickens see in the dark? Chickens can't see very well in the dark, which is why nocturnal predators have so much luck getting them at night.

What is the difference between fertilized and unfertilized eggs? Is one "more healthy" to eat than the other? They look the same inside and out and taste the same. The fertile egg will contain a minute piece of sperm from the male and, when placed in ideal heat and humidity for twenty-one days, will form a chick.

Under what conditions or social pressures will a chicken fight another chicken? Males fight for territorial rights, especially if females are near. Any birds in a crowded space will fight to get feed or water.

Under what conditions will a chicken peck at another chicken? To show dominance or to defend themselves, chickens will peck at one another.

Will my chickens be tame if I work with them? Yes. Some breeds are naturally quiet and calm, but all birds benefit from daily handling and human contact.

How do I avoid a rooster attack? Always move slowly and calmly. Don't stand between a rooster and his hens. If you are attacked, try not to run, but turn and defend yourself with a kick toward the rooster or use a stick to fend off the bird. You need to let him know you are dominant.

What if a rooster chases me? Stop; don't run. Face it and be ready to kick it away. A stick or pole can also be used to fend off the bird. A rooster that attacks you once will do it again. Consider culling the bird if he continually attacks you or others.

Can I bring a chicken in the house like a pet? It can be done. Chickens are not house-trainable, but diapers are available. Remember that chickens are social and prefer the company of other chickens. The floors in your house can also be too slippery for birds.

How often do chickens lose their feathers or "molt?" Adult birds drop their feathers and replace them with new ones once a year. Hens stop laying during this time due to the need for extra protein to form the new feathers.

How do I wash eggs? Wash them with a little dish soap and water at room temperature. Soak them in the dishwater for a few minutes, wipe gently with a terry-cloth rag, and air-dry on a towel before placing in an egg carton.

What do I need to know if I sell eggs? Regulations, freshness, and cleanliness are the top three things you will need to know.

How can I tell if an egg is past its prime? Place the eggs in a bucket of water. Eggs that are old will float because of gas buildup inside the shell.

How do I get large or small eggs? Breed is the primary consideration for determining egg size. Hens also tend to lay larger eggs as they age.

What parts of the chicken can be eaten? What do I do with the rest? Most of the internal organs, feathers, feet, and head are considered waste and should be incinerated or buried in a deep hole to prevent predator problems. The skin, body, gizzard, liver, and heart are all edible.

What if I find I can't take care of my chickens? What do I do with them? First check your state's regulations with regard to selling of livestock. Start by asking another poultry enthusiast, or post ads at the local feed mill. Attend a chicken swap to sell your chickens or butcher them for home use.

ACQUIRING CHICKENS

C hickens are social creatures with a "pecking order," which means exactly that. One bird is dominant, is first at the feed trough, and has the best roosting spot. Another may hide in a corner, be last to leave the coop, and may be bullied. Each bird has its own unique temperament. If care is used in choosing flockmates, birds fighting and being picked on can be avoided for an overall happier and healthier flock. Knowing the specific characteristics of each breed as mentioned in the *American Standard of Perfection*, as well as temperament and compatibility with other breeds, is especially important if you plan on keeping more than one breed of chickens.

A nice-sized backyard flock consists of twenty-four hens and one rooster. This rooster appears to be a silver-penciled Rock, and the hens are predominately silver-laced Wyandottes and buff Orpingtons with a few Easter-egg layers. The eggs from this flock will be in shades of brown and blue-greens.
Corallina Breuer

Purebred versus Crossbred

Purebred means a bird's genes all come from a single breed. Crossbred means that a bird's genetic makeup includes genes of more than one breed. You can choose to raise crossbred or purebred birds. A combination of both may be suitable if care is used when selecting the breed types in areas like size and aggression.

Purebreds have been raised and developed for specific uses, characteristics, and temperaments. Many purebred breeds you find today were entered in the *American Standard of Perfection* more than a hundred years ago. Their genetics have stood the test of time, and they have remained popular enough with chicken keepers to be admired still and raised in today's hobby, whether they are being exhibited or kept in a backyard flock. Mate a purebred rooster and a purebred hen of the same breed and variety, and all the resulting offspring should look and act alike. This is useful if you choose to raise your own birds as a later project.

Purebreds are usually a better choice for a youth project, especially if you plan to exhibit your birds. County fairs have divisions based on a bird's age, sex, classification, breed, and sometimes variety. You won't fit into one of these divisions if you're raising and showing crossbred birds. Purebreds offer many other advantages, including uniform size and unique traits that have been developed for a specific use, such as the extremely small comb in the Canadian-bred Chantecler that allows for better cold-weather tolerance.

Crossbred birds, also referred to as hybrids, offer some advantages. Most commercial hatcheries offer egg-laying crosses in white and brown egg-layers. These hens can be great additions to a large fowl flock by providing a steady, plentiful supply of eggs. Your county fair may even have a specific show class for them. Crossbred birds are not part of the *American Standard of Perfection*

This young buff Wyandotte cockerel has the rich buff color of his variety plus the red earlobe and rose comb of the Wyandotte breed. Buff Wyandottes were admitted to the *American Standard of Perfection* in 1901. Other varieties of this breed in large fowl and bantam include silver-laced, golden-laced, white, black, blue, partridge silver-penciled, and Columbian. The bantam division also recognizes buff Columbian. *DeAnn Richards*

> Purebreds have been raised and developed for specific uses, characteristics, and temperaments. Their genetics have stood the test of time, and they have remained popular enough with chicken keepers to be admired still.

This show-quality silver-penciled Rock bantam cock is in excellent condition. Use your thumb to cover his head in this picture and notice how the pointed feathers on his hackle and saddle areas clearly indicate this is a male without having to look at the comb. *Corallina Breuer*

matings. Know the characteristics of each breed before you attempt to mix them. You don't want to create a crossbred chicken that will lack needed characteristics on your farm. A hatching project, whether done in an incubator or naturally using a broody hen, can be a very rewarding and educational project. Calculating the days until hatching, caring for the special needs of the broody hen, and maintaining the proper incubator environment all make for great chicken-keeping experiences! The same work and costs are involved for purebred or crossbred matings, and crossbreds eat as much as purebreds, so you might want to save your feed and only raise the types of birds that will be the most beneficial to you.

> The same work and costs are involved for purebred or crossbred matings, but a crossbred chick hatch brings fewer benefits to you.

This cock is an example of a sex-linked hybrid cross. All the females from this strain of bird are rich cinnamon in color with a few cream feathers mixed in. The males have a creamy white base with a few red feathers on their chests and wings. The male and female chicks are also colored differently, which makes them easy for hatcheries to sex. *Corallina Breuer*

and will not have a class at any APA show, however. Judges at county fairs judge these birds on overall health and feather condition only. Crossbred chickens aren't able to move up to champion row to compete against purebred fowl.

You can develop crossbreds by mating a purebred rooster and a purebred hen of a different breed or variety. The resulting offspring may look like either parent, look like a mix of the two, or look totally different than either parent depending on the combined breeds. Use restraint and make careful choices before conducting random

Experienced poultry breeders experiment with crosses for several reasons. They may want to develop a new purebred type, increase vigor in their flock, or fine-tune a specific characteristic in a chosen breed. All of these cross-matings take several generations of careful selection to obtain offspring to breed for the next generation. Extensive record-keeping must be used throughout the process, and genetic knowledge of the breed characteristics is needed to predict the desired outcome. Poultry breeders have multiple breeding pens, keep large numbers of birds, and are willing to invest many years and often a lot of money into these experiments. Unless you are able to make that much of a commitment, leave the crossbred matings to others.

This is a grouping of 4-H show birds. Notice the deep, rich red on the rose-comb Rhode Island pullet and the nice size and coloring on the pair of black Australorp pullets. The back cockerel is a young partridge Cochin that will take a little more time to fully develop. *Kendall Babcock*

This pair of salmon Faverolle bantam hens shows the deeper, broader carriage of the breed. The hen on the left is a great example of what is desired in the breed. Both exhibit the desired creamy white beard and muffs, and both should also have fifth toes. Males in this variety are a much different color. *Corallina Breuer*

Bantam versus Large Fowl

There are two basic chicken sizes: bantam or large fowl. Unless you are able to have two or more separate coops or pens, choose only one basic size of bird. There are advantages and disadvantages to both sizes. Keep the following points in mind when choosing what size bird you are going to raise.

Egg Production

Bantams are generally seasonal layers with good egg-laying spurts in late spring through early fall. Many large fowl hens, especially the Mediterranean breeds, lay consistently year-round when given adequate shelter and extra lighting to eliminate seasonal shortcomings of natural sunlight. If you want to supply your family or others with eggs, large fowl birds may be a better choice for you. On the other hand, if you are less concerned with eggs and are looking for fun-loving little birds, you may enjoy a bantam flock.

Egg Size

Bantam eggs, like bantam chickens themselves, are much smaller than the large- to jumbo-graded size you find in the grocery store. It generally takes three to four bantam eggs to equal the size of two large-graded eggs, but the amount of feed used by bantam hens to produce eggs is at a better conversion rate than it is with their large fowl counterparts. Therefore, egg size may not be a reason to avoid the bantam breeds if you are

This splash Andalusian pullet enjoys the protection of some tall weeds along with a white-faced black Spanish cockerel. The splash color results from crossing blue-to-blue color genes. In a true blue-to-blue mating, 25 percent of the chicks will be black, 25 percent of the chicks will be splash, and 50 percent will be blue. *DeAnn Richards*

29

These three different breeds of large fowl hens get along well both in the coop and free-range. The hens are a silver-laced Wyandotte, a hybrid egg-laying breed, and a commercial red Rhode Island. Commercial means she doesn't have the rich mahogany red color of good show stock. All these breeds lay brown eggs. *Corallina Breuer*

willing to eat a six-egg bantam omelet instead of the standard three-egg omelet. Large fowl eggs, depending on the breed, may be smaller than the grocery store eggs because the purchased eggs were produced by hens that are a commercial cross and specifically bred to produce many uniform large eggs in a short lifespan. You will probably keep your hens for several years and can expect smaller eggs when they first start laying. Their eggs may get larger than the jumbo grocery store eggs as your hens get older.

Coop Size

Coop size depends on your yard size and the number of chickens in your flock. Square footage requirements per bird vary by breed. A mature large fowl bird generally needs 2 to 2.5 square feet per bird. A mature bantam bird needs 1 to 1.5 square feet per bird. In order to calculate coop space, measure the width and depth of your coop's floor area,

multiply the measurements, and divide the total by either 2.25 or 1.25. The resulting number tells you how many birds of each size can happily live in your coop. Make minor number adjustments based on final breed selection and size. You can obviously have more birds if you keep bantams and less if you choose large fowl.

Breed Choices

All purebred breeds of chickens have bantam varieties. However, not all breeds come in a large fowl version. Silkies and Sebrights are two examples of breeds that are bantam only. If you decide on bantam-only breeds, you have made a choice to keep bantams and therefore should limit your purchases to that size of chicken.

Dual-Purpose Birds

A dual-purpose bird is equally suited for egg and meat production. If you plan to butcher

This Modern Game cockerel in the brown-red color variety is the diminutive leader of a large flock. His long legs, large eyes, and spirited nature keep him in on all the action in the poultry yard. Note he is not dubbed (comb and wattles trimmed close to the head), which is a requirement for showing cocks in his class. *Kelly Damaschke*

excess roosters and cull hens for meat uses, a large fowl breed is much better suited to your needs. The carcass size for your time and the production costs involved creates a much better ratio than with bantams. Either way, you'll need to rid your flock of excess roosters and cull hens. A dual-purpose large fowl breed, such as Rocks, Wyandottes, or

Delawares, should be considered if you are looking at meat to offset some of your costs.

Chick Purchasing Options

You will most likely be getting straight-run birds if you purchase chicks from a private breeder. Straight-run means "as hatched," which is ideally 50 percent pullets

The lack of barbs on each feather makes Silkies appear to have hair instead of feathers. This trait also keeps the sex feathering from showing on the Silkie males. You will need to use extra caution when purchasing young adults of this breed to be sure of the sex of the birds. *Tara Kindschi*

Chickens running in your backyard may make you smile. The classic sight of a barred Plymouth Rock hen brings joy to new and old-time poultry enthusiasts alike. This traditional dual-purpose American breed is a good choice to start your flock if you are unsure of what breed you'll like. *Shelly Sonsalla*

These two bearded white Polish chickens clearly show the difference in sex feathers. It is very easy to sex birds based on something other than comb development. The female's crest feathers are all curved and form a soft topknot while the male's crest has the pointed feathers that form more of a punk hair look. Both birds show good feather condition and have the crest size of show-quality stock. *Corallina Breuer*

Pet carriers work well for transporting chickens. They can be purchased at most pet stores and are usually sized for cats and dogs. Get the size that allows your birds to stand without touching the ceiling. The plastic bottoms can be slippery for birds, so it's a good idea to create a thick bed with wood shavings. *Tara Kindschi*

and 50 percent cockerels. Mother Nature and genetics play a role, however, and the extremes of 80 to 20 percent of each sex can often be found in a single hatch. Commercial hatcheries sometimes offer all-pullet or all-cockerel chicks. These chicks are sexed at hatching and sold by sex with a 90 to 95 percent accuracy rate. You pay more for the pullets, but you'll feed fewer birds and don't have to deal with excess roosters if you are planning for a laying flock. Unfortunately, many large fowl breeds and most bantam breeds are not offered as pullets only for two reasons. The first reason is that excess males in a smaller breed have no economic value, and if the hatcheries can't sell them, they must

be destroyed, so they take a little less money to sell straight-run and are therefore able to sell everything. The second reason is that sexing a day-old chick is a very specialized science that only a few people do, and not all hatcheries have a chick-sexer on staff. If you are concerned about becoming emotionally attached to what will become "excess roosters" as your birds age, consider starting with a selection of pullets only.

Showing and Transporting

Until you determine your personal preference for showing, start with a smaller, calmer hen for a beginning showmanship bird. A bird that is calm, stays steady in small hands, and is easy to move, lift, turn, and wash is the best choice for a show bird. Daily handling and a quiet, calm demeanor when you are around your flock will result in almost any bird being calmer. Also, a smaller bird needs a smaller cage or pet carrier for transport to the shows.

If you prefer a large bird for its eggs and still want to show, be prepared to work harder to be able to handle your bird properly for showmanship. You'll also need bigger carriers and transport space for large fowl.

Chicks versus Adult Birds

There is nothing cuter in the world than a day-old fuzzy chick peeping and looking up at you. Make sure you have established a plan before you buy any chicks. A spur-of-the-moment purchase of chicks when you happen to see them at the local feed store can leave you with a type of bird you don't want for the long term. The same can be said for acquiring adult birds or chicks simply from how nice they look in the *American Standard of Perfection* illustration. Goals must be determined before

you become responsible for raising a flock of chickens.

The time of year can be a large factor in what chickens are available for purchase. In spring and early summer, hatcheries and private breeders offer many chick breed choices. You may not find chicks from a breeder in late fall, since they tend to hatch their chicks in the spring and use their limited space to raise the chicks into adults. Fall is

This day-old blue Cochin large fowl chick already exhibits the wide stance and deep body structure of the Cochin breed. The downy shanks and outer and middle toes indicate this bird will have the intense leg feathering of a good-quality Cochin.
Tara Kindschi

Advantages of Buying Chicks

- Less expensive per bird
- Ship easily at less cost
- Easy to find hatcheries

Advantages of Buying Adult Birds

- You know how they'll look as adults
- Egg production and showing can start right away
- Breeding program can start right away
- Immediately can go into your coop

Disadvantages of Buying Chicks

- Require special care for eight-plus weeks
- Sex unknown unless sexed at hatchery
- May lose some in the growing process

Disadvantages of Buying Adult Birds

- Expensive to ship
- Higher cost per bird
- May not be tame
- May have bad habits

usually when the breeders selectively cull their birds, keep breeders and show birds, and offer the rest for sale. These culled birds may have serious defects and be unsuitable for you, or they may lack a bit in size or coloring but still develop into a nice bird for your flock. Take your time, refer to the *American Standard of Perfection*, and ask a lot of questions before you make a final selection. The advantage to buying adult birds is you can more easily see what they are going to become when they are older.

Pullets and cockerels are not your only choice in adult birds. Some breeders may have slightly older birds they are culling that can be a good purchase if you are sure the birds aren't older than two years, look healthy, and have no obvious defects.

Most breeders keep a limited number of birds for breeding and showing through the winter, so no extra adult birds may be available in early spring. Many hatcheries offer chicks year-round, but you may have to wait longer for a hatch to be set. Shipping chicks in the dead of winter can be risky. Only a few hatcheries offer started birds (eight to ten weeks of age) due to increased shipping costs and restrictions. These birds are usually

A trio of large fowl, buff Orpington hens exhibits the buff color often seen in commercial breeding stock. Show-stock birds have a richer, more even color over the entire body. When showing birds like these, protect them from direct sunlight, since they are very prone to color fading. *Kelly Damaschke*

This young, non-bearded, buff, laced Polish appears to be a pullet due to the lack of growth in its comb and wattles, but its final feathers are not in yet, so it could be a late-maturing cockerel. In either case, the crest of feathers appears quite sparse. This bird probably does not have enough crest formation to be of show quality. *Tara Kindschi*

handled on a pick-up-only basis. Scout out the hatcheries within driving distance of your home for any that may offer started birds as an option.

Breeder versus Commercial Hatchery

Commercial hatcheries offer chicks year-round on the date you specify and in the quantity of each breed you desire. Breeders may not be able to do that quite as well.

Many breeders have invested years of work in fine-tuning a breed or breeds and are more than happy to pass on their knowledge along with your bird purchase. Many breed clubs can be found on the Internet, or you can meet breeders in person by attending an APA or American Bantam Association (ABA) poultry show. Poultry newsletters and magazines like *Backyard Poultry* and the *Poultry Press* are good sources for information about upcoming shows and what breeders live in your area. Also refer to the breed clubs listing in the resources section of this book.

Breeders will commonly sell unsexed chicks or adult birds. Prices may seem higher than for hatchery chicks, but you are often able to see the parent birds, find out what awards this line of birds has won, and learn more from the breeder about showing and general care tips for a particular breed.

This large fowl, white-laced, red Cornish hen exhibits excellent feather condition but is a poor type for her breed. Her coloring is not distinct, her breast and overall body are both too narrow, and her head is too fine. Standard varieties include buff, white, and white-laced red in large fowl, plus black, mottled, spangled, and blue-laced red in bantam. *Tara Kindschi*

Many breeders only sell adult birds. While this can be confusing and frustrating for a starting bird enthusiast, their reasoning is two-fold. Most breeders don't want to sell you an inferior bird. Not all chicks will turn out to be great birds. Breeders hatch limited numbers of birds (they also have space and time limitations) and must be sure to have enough quality birds to continue their line of genetics. Breeders will gladly sell extra adult birds if they have them. The timing may not be as ideal as reserving an order through a commercial hatchery, but the rewards can be well worth it in the quality of your bird.

As you gain more experience, you may want to experiment to see what offers you the best quality birds for your investment. Your results will vary by region, the variety you choose, and how you raise the birds.

These two pens of non-bearded, white-crested, black Polish are being offered for sale in the swap area at an APA–sanctioned show. Notice the use of the add-on feeder for supplying the birds with feed while in these cages. These types of feeders are available for purchase from many poultry supply stores. *Tara Kindschi*

CHOOSING A BREED

A frizzle white Cochin bantam cockerel shows how the frizzle gene can be genetically applied to any breed of chicken. Frizzle is most often seen in loose-feathered breeds of bantams, such as the Cochin. Extra care needs to be taken when mating, since two frizzle parents can produce offspring that are "over frizzled," which results in the feathers curling so much that they break at the skin, which leaves an unprotected, basically unfeathered bird.
Kendall Babcock

IN THIS SECTION

There is so much diversity in chicken breeds! It can be overwhelming to look at pictures of all the choices and read the unusual names. How do you ever decide on a breed that is suitable for you? Looks and habits will help you narrow down your options. Just remember to stay with all bantams (small fowl) or all large fowl. You can mix and match the breeds to suit multiple needs and interests important to you and your family.

Considerations When Picking a Breed

- Looks
- Habits
- Size
- Variety
- Unusual Qualities
- Usefulness

Considerations When Picking Breeds to Show

- Unique Physical Traits
- Show Class
- General Temperament

Varieties within breeds are often reflected in color patterns or comb style differences within a base breed. A rose comb versus a single comb variety may be better for colder climates. A solid-colored bird, such as black or white, is easier to perfect and tends to place better at shows than a speckled or mottled version. Certain varieties may be rare and therefore less available for purchase. As you make your selections, plan to make a few choices within each breed. Refer to the complete breed listing that follows to see the many varieties within breeds. You'll be able to establish which breeds are best to handle, are fun to look at, are easy to show, are good egg-layers, or produce the best meat from the following information.

A black Sumatra in show condition is an impressive, elegant sight to behold. This cock exhibits a nice tail sweep and good overall coloring. Closer inspection is needed to see if he has the desired multiple-spur trait and the yellow-bottomed feet of the Sumatra standard. *Corallina Breuer*

Cuddlers

Are you looking for a pet you can hold and cuddle? Calm, easy-going birds (that may also be picked on by more aggressive flockmates) include Cochins and Faverolles in large fowl. Silkies, Orpingtons, and Wyandottes are the bantam breeds of this demeanor. Most of these breeds make great broody hens.

Crested Breeds

Want to turn heads with those unusual-looking wild hairdos? Consider crested breeds like Polish, Sultans, Crevecoeurs, and Silkies. Temperaments vary by breed and sex, but all require special care to keep that topknot of feathers looking nice. These breeds don't see as well and have a hard time avoiding predators. Certain feeders and waterers can cause food particle buildup on the head feathers. The extra head feathers are also hard for the bird to keep clean, and mites can linger there.

A 4-H member cuddles one of her pet birds. She raises many breeds of chickens in large fowl and bantam. This black Cochin bantam hen is a calm, friendly bird, which is quite common for the breed. *Kendall Babcock*

This is an impressive view of a non-bearded, white-crested, black Polish cock's crest and head. His eyes and comb appear to be completely hidden by his crest feathers. To obtain this level of feather quality, this bird is housed in a breeding pen that contains only him and two females. Both his waterer and feeder are open containers to keep his crest from rubbing or getting dirtied by standard equipment. *Kendall Babcock*

This light Brahma large fowl hen is a member of the Asiatic class, which also includes Cochins and Langshans. All three breeds originated in Asia, as the class name suggests, and all have varying numbers of feathers on their shanks and toes. *Tara Kindschi*

Feathers Everywhere! (Even the Legs)

Feathers everywhere is what it's all about. Breeds with more feathers in both large fowl and bantam sizes include Cochins, Brahmas, Langshans, and Faverolles. Bantam breeds like the Belgian Bearded d'Uccle Bantam and the Booted Bantam, as well as Silkies, are also included in this category.

Brown Egg versus White Egg

What color will she lay? Check a chicken's earlobe to determine her egg color. If a hen has a whitish blue earlobe, she will always lay a pure white egg. One with a red earlobe will lay a colored egg. She will usually produce brown but could also produce the shades of blue or green found in the South American

breeds like the Ameraucanas. Brown eggs can be the light tan of a Sussex breed or the deep chocolate color of a Maran. A hen will lay the same color of egg her entire life. Genetics, not environment, determine eggshell color.

Fancy Egg Colors

Want more than just white and brown eggs from your flock? What about blues and greens and chocolates? Marans, Welsummers, and Barnevelders are all known for deep, dark, rich brown eggs. Ameraucanas and Araucanas lay shades of blue-green to green eggs.

Hardworking Egg-Layers

Are you looking for a purebred breed that lays and lays? Choose the white Leghorns that originated in the Mediterranean. These hens are generally non-broody, white egg-layers known for frugal yet superb egg production. It is common for one hen to lay over three hundred eggs a year! All varieties of Leghorns and Anconas are good white egg-layers. Delawares, Rhode Islands, and Marans are good choices for brown eggs.

A light-brown Leghorn pullet enjoys foraging on a late winter day. This view shows her streamlined Leghorn body and the rich coloring of the light-brown variety. Notice her white earlobes, which indicate she lays white eggs. *Kendall Babcock*

A cuckoo Maran hen enjoys the shade under an apple tree on a hot summer day. The Maran is a breed of bird gaining popularity for its rich-brown (almost chocolate) egg color. Other breeds known for rich-brown eggs include Barnevelders and Welsummers. *Corallina Breuer*

Chickens are a great size of an animal for youth to own. This large fowl, barred Plymouth Rock hen enjoys being handled and has been to many shows and petting zoos. She is a good example of her breed. *Tara Kindschi*

The unique-looking Modern Game shown here is a Birchen bantam version. Notice the poor tail feather condition on the male and that he has not been dubbed (trimmed comb and wattles), which is a requirement for cock birds in the Modern Game class. *Corallina Breuer*

Dual-Purpose Breeds

What about a breed that does just about everything? Delawares, Australorps, Buckeyes, and Javas would be good additions to your flock. They lay well, the carcass size is suitable for meat production, they are great free-rangers, and they can handle cold climates.

Endangered Breeds

Want to help save rare heritage breeds from becoming extinct? The American Livestock Breeds Conservancy lists the following chicken breeds as critical: Andalusian, Aseel, Buckeye, Buttercup, Campine, Catalana, Chantecler, Crevecoeur, Delaware, Faverolle, Holland, Houdan, La Fleche, Malay, Nankin, Redcap, Russian Orloff, Spanish, and Sumatra. The critical status means there are fewer than five hundred breeding birds

in the United States, there are five or fewer primary breeding flocks (fifty birds or more), and the birds are considered globally endangered.

Just Plain Oddballs

Want a truly unique sight? "Naked Neck" is the common name for the Turkens breed. The name tells you everything; they have no feathers on their necks and fewer feathers than most breeds on the rest of their bodies.

The extremely long-legged Modern Game breed is very attractive and popular at shows. The Silkie, with its black skin and bones and feathers that look like fluff, is a great bantam-only breed.

The Java is a rare breed currently listed as threatened by the American Livestock Breeds Conservancy. Javas can be found in black and mottled and are considered an early dual-purpose breed in the American class. This day-old chick is a black Java. *Tara Kindschi*

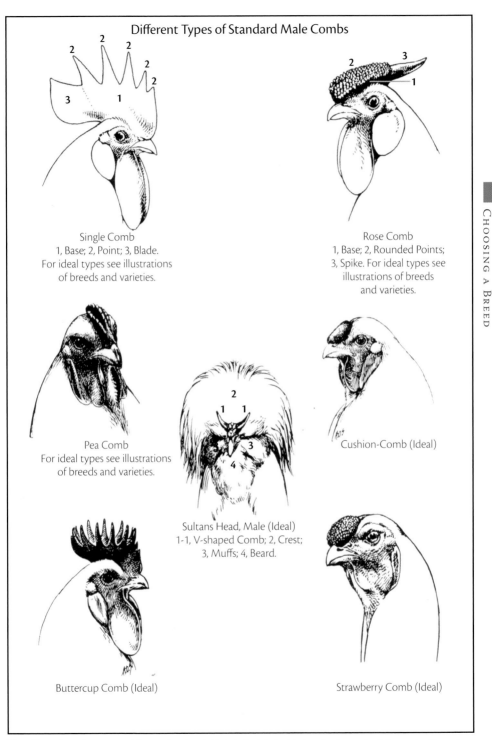

Different Types of Standard Male Combs

Single Comb
1, Base; 2, Point; 3, Blade.
For ideal types see illustrations
of breeds and varieties.

Rose Comb
1, Base; 2, Rounded Points;
3, Spike. For ideal types see
illustrations of breeds
and varieties.

Pea Comb
For ideal types see illustrations
of breeds and varieties.

Sultans Head, Male (Ideal)
1-1, V-shaped Comb; 2, Crest;
3, Muffs; 4, Beard.

Cushion-Comb (Ideal)

Buttercup Comb (Ideal)

Strawberry Comb (Ideal)

These illustrations show seven of the comb styles of chickens. Each is the ideal version in a male of the species. The styles represented include: single, rose, pea, V-shaped, cushion, buttercup, and strawberry. Refer to these pictures when trying to identify adults or chicks. *Reprinted from the American Standard of Perfection with permission from the APA*

Many purebred and crossbred breeds of chickens make excellent layers for the backyard flock. This is a non-standard-color Ameraucana often sold by hatcheries as an Easter-egg hen. They are great layers, are adequate mothers, and come in a variety of colors, all with muffs. Buying standard colors from breeders is the best option if you would like to exhibit this breed. *Kendall Babcock*

Complete Breed Listing

This section includes a list of all the purebred breeds of chicken available in the United States. Some of these breeds are not featured in the American Poultry Association's *American Standard of Perfection* but can be purchased from hatcheries and breeders. Use the following list to help you make a good selection for breed and variety that is based not only on looks (pictures in a hatchery catalog), but also on where the breed fits in show classes, any unique physical traits, and general temperament.

Ameraucana: These are chickens that lay green- or blue-tinted eggs and have muffs, a beard, no ear tufts, and a pea comb. Standard colors include white, blue, blue wheaton, brown/red, buff, silver, wheaton, and black. This breed shows in the All Other Standard Breeds class as large fowl and All Other Comb Clean Leg class as bantams. Many hatcheries sell these birds as "Easter-egg layers" that are bred for egg color only, so don't plan on showing birds described as such. Birds from

any source that sells this breed without a color named are probably not show quality.

Ancona: This is a Mediterranean-class large fowl, a white-egg-layer, and a hardy bird that takes its name from the city of Ancona, Italy. Both single and rose comb versions have been bred. These birds feature black plumage with some feathers tipped with white, and a lopped single comb is required for exhibition hens. Bantams show in the Clean Leg Single or Rose Comb divisions.

Andalusian (Blue): A graceful bird from Spain, this large white-egg-layer is a non-setter. It can be a difficult breed to work with, as black and splash-colored chicks are always produced from blue-bird matings, though only the blues can be shown. The other black and splash birds make great layers or breeders. Large fowl show as Mediterranean class birds, and bantams show as Single Comb Clean Leg birds.

Araucana: Rumpless (tailless) and ear-tufted birds originally bred in South America, these are very hard to find in the United

States. They are also known for laying blue eggs, and they show in the All Other Standard Breeds class as large fowl and All Other Combs Clean Leg class for bantam versions. The breed carries a gene that causes many chicks to die during incubation, so expect these birds to be more expensive and not stocked by many commercial hatcheries.

Aseel: These are ancestors to the Cornish breed, but they look more slender and athletic than Cornish birds. Heavy-boned, heavy-muscled, and very hard-feathered birds (bare breastbone) with an upright carriage, they feature a small pea comb and an unusual eye color mix of white and green. The birds' sloping tails tend to fan, and the hens are poor layers but tenacious setters. A drawback to birds of this breed is that they were originally bred for fighting, and they will constantly fight among themselves (both males and females) if not given plenty of room to roam. Colors include black-breasted red, dark, spangled, and white, but only the wheaten female Aseels are part of the *American Standard of Perfection.*

Australorp: Developed in Australia from Orpingtons, these birds have an easy-going temperament and good egg production of tinted brown/rose eggs. They are good-sized large fowl birds; cocks weigh about 8 ½ pounds. Black with a greenish sheen to their plumage, they show in the English class for large fowl and the Single Comb Clean Leg for bantams.

Barnevelder: This Dutch breed lays a very dark-brown egg and includes white, black, and blue-laced varieties. The birds have calm temperaments, and they are a good choice for the backyard flock keeper looking for a dark egg color. The breed shows in the Continental class as a large fowl.

Belgian Bearded d'Anvers Bantam: A true bantam, there are no large fowl counterparts. The birds are bearded, and

colors include black, mottled, porcelain, self blue, and quail. Males are aggressive toward humans, but hens make great, calm little pets. The breed shows in the bantam Rose Comb Clean Leg class.

Belgian Bearded d'Uccle Bantam: A true bantam, this is the bearded version of the Booted Bantam. Colors include mille fleur, porcelain, mottled, self blue, and others. These single-combed birds show as Feathered-Leg bantams. The *American Standard of Perfection* calls for vulture hocks, which result in a disqualification in most other breeds. Be aware that because chickens of this variety are very gentle, more aggressive birds may pick on them.

This Brabanter pullet is very pretty and a rare breed in the United States. She shows good body condition and appears comfortable in her cage. *Corallina Breuer*

Booted Bantam: This is a bantam-only breed with booted feet. A non-bearded version of the Belgian Bearded D'Uccle breed, its standard colors include black, mille fleur, porcelain, self blue, and white. The *American Standard of Perfection* calls for vulture hocks, which result in a disqualification in most other breeds.

Brabanter: This is an old Dutch breed with a peculiar comb ending in two V-shaped horns. Colors include black, blue, white, cuckoo, gold, silver, and chamois. Though some hatcheries sell these, they are currently not accepted in the *American Standard of Perfection* and cannot earn awards at an APA-sanctioned show.

Brahma: A huge, regal, large fowl bird, this breed comes in three recognized varieties of light, buff, and dark. Commercial hatchery birds are smaller in stature than good show stock, so take extra care and view parents before making a purchase. Calm, easy-going birds with a small comb that resists frostbite, they show in the Asiatic class for large fowl and Feathered Leg class for bantams.

Buckeye: Admitted to the *American Standard of Perfection* in 1904 in the American class for large fowl, these were developed in the Buckeye State of Ohio as a dual-purpose breed with the distinctive color of the buckeye nut, a glowing deep red. They have a gentle nature and a pea comb, and the bantams show in the All Other Comb Clean Leg class.

Campine: Developed in Belgium for white egg production, this breed comes in silver and golden varieties, both with a very pretty barring-type pattern. These chickens tend to be independent, flighty birds, and the males are often aggressive toward humans. The breed is entered in the Continental class in large fowl and Single Comb Clean Leg class in bantams.

Catalana (Buff): Accepted into the *American Standard of Perfection* in 1949, this Spanish breed was primarily grown as a meat bird. Buff-colored with a black tail, it is considered a rare breed in the United States. Hens lay a large white egg, and the huge comb with six points is often hard to maintain in cold temperatures. Large fowl of this breed are part of the Mediterranean class, and bantams are part of the Single Comb Clean Leg class.

Chantecler: This breed originated in the colder climate of Canada, so the birds are strong, calm fowl and good winter layers. They also have small combs and wattles less prone to frostbite. Colors include white, buff, and partridge, and the breed shows in the American class for large fowl and the All Other Comb Clean Leg class for bantams.

This is a silver-laced Wyandotte bantam hen. Average weights for bantam Wyandottes are 30 ounces for a cock and 26 ounces for a hen versus 8.5 pounds for a large fowl cock and 6.5 pounds for a large fowl hen. This is quite a size difference! *Tara Kindschi*

Cochin: The Cochin is a huge chicken; a large fowl cock of this breed can weigh up to 11 pounds, with hens at 8 ½ pounds. And thick, fluffy feathers and feathered legs make them look even bigger. Colors include buff, partridge, white, black, silver-laced, gold-laced, blue, red/brown, and barred. Originating in China, the easy-going disposition of these birds makes them a great choice for youth to raise in either size. Both large fowl and bantams are good setters, and they show in the Asiatic class for large fowl and the Feathered Leg class for the bantams.

Cornish: Developed in Cornwall, England, this hard-feathered breed has a small pea comb and is pretty unique looking, with fairly short legs set wide apart under a huge breast and heavy body. Most modern-day broiler crosses are a result of mating Cornish chickens to Plymouth Rock chickens for the extreme fast growth and weight gain of hybrids. Colors include white, dark, white-laced red, and buff. Bantams show as All Other Comb Clean Leg birds, and large fowl fit the English class.

Crevecoeur: This French breed has a lustrous green-black plumage and V-comb. One of the rarest crested breeds, the birds show in the Continental class as large fowl and All Other Comb Clean Leg as bantam.

Cubalaya: From the Oriental division in the All Other Standard Breeds large fowl class, this breed was developed in Cuba and is very "gamey" looking with a short beak and head and a pea comb. It is recognized in colors of black-breasted red, black, and white. Bantams show in the All Other Comb Clean Leg class, and the birds' looks and habits are much like the original jungle fowl from which all other domestic breeds of chickens originated.

Delaware: This American breed was developed in Delaware in the 1940s and is considered dual-purpose. The birds lay brown eggs and grow very fast. White with barring

on only the tail and hackle, the breed shows in the American class for large fowl and the Single Comb Clean Leg class for bantam.

Dominique: A rare American breed found in the barred pattern, these birds are good foragers with a rose comb and are slightly smaller in size than Plymouth Rocks. They show as large fowl in the American class and in the Rose Comb Clean Leg class as a bantam.

Dorking: A heavy chicken with a large, square frame, this breed matures slowly and is an excellent forager. Available in single or rose comb, the birds always have a fifth toe, and colors include silver-gray, colored, red, and white. They show in the large fowl English class and the bantam Rose Comb or Single Comb Clean Leg classes, depending on the comb.

Dutch Bantam: Among the smallest bantams, with cocks weighing 21 ounces and hens 19 ounces, these birds are available in many colors, including three standard: light brown, silver, and blue/light brown. The birds show in the Single Comb Clean Leg class.

Egyptian Fayoumi: These are small, active chickens that mature very fast. Pullets may start laying a small egg by four months of age, and cockerels will often be crowing by six weeks. The plumage pattern is similar to that of the Campine, and though they are flighty birds, they aren't aggressive to people and are excellent foragers. This breed is not yet listed in the *American Standard of Perfection*.

Faverolle: A French breed developed in the 1850s as a utility bird, the standard colors for the Faverolle are white and salmon. Salmon-colored males are more colorful than the females and can be sexed at a few weeks of age by their color. Unique traits for this breed include a calm demeanor, feathered legs, and a fifth toe. The breed shows in the Continental class for large fowl and Feathered Leg class for bantams.

A silver-spangled Hamburg cock enjoys looking for bugs and greens on an early summer day. This breed is known as an ornamental non-setting breed that lays white eggs. The Hamburg also comes in golden-spangled, golden-penciled, silver-penciled, white, and black. All have rose combs. *Corallina Breuer*

Hamburg: A rose comb breed that comes in more than ten varieties, including penciled and spangled colors as well as solids, these birds are attractive in hatchery catalogs and great for white eggs. This is a very stately bird that shows in the Continental class for large fowl and Single Comb Clean Leg for bantams.

Holland: A heavy, dual-purpose breed that lays white eggs, the Holland chicken was admitted to the *American Standard of Perfection* in 1949. Colors are barred and white, and this can be a rare bird at shows. Bantams would fit the Single Comb Clean Leg class, and the large fowl fits in the American class.

A small group of black-tailed white Japanese bantams enjoy foraging in the shade on a hot summer day. These birds clearly exhibit the unique squirrel tail and extremely short legs of the Japanese breed. This breed has several other varieties, such as mottled, black-tailed buff, wheaten, white, brown-red, and gray. *Kelly Damaschke*

Houdan: This is an old French breed known for its fine meat and large, white eggs. Unique characteristics include a large crest, fifth toe, and V-shaped comb, and colors include mottled and white. The bird shows in the Continental class for large fowl and the All Other Comb Clean Leg class for bantam.

Iowa Blue: A bird in a gray pencil pattern rather than a blue bird as the name implies, this breed was developed in Decorah, Iowa, to be a good forager and setter. However, it does not appear in the *American Standard of Perfection*.

Japanese Bantam: A true bantam with no large fowl counterpart, the breed occurs in various colors including black-tailed white, black, mottled, black-tailed buff, and gray. These birds have very short, clean legs and cause little damage to lawns and gardens. The breed fits the bantam class of Single Comb Clean Leg, and its unique tail structure (called a squirrel tail) results in disqualification in other breeds.

Java: A slow-growing, dual-purpose breed that lays brown eggs, its colors include black and mottled. The Java breed shows in the American class for large fowl and the Single Comb Clean Leg class for bantam.

This black Jersey Giant cock is as much of a pet as livestock for this young owner. The bird has been handled daily since it was a chick and is unafraid in human surroundings. It is an ideal choice for a showmanship bird because it is mature, is in good body and feather condition, and is calm and manageable despite its large size. *DeAnn Richards*

Jersey Giant: A giant large fowl chicken with cocks weighing 13 pounds and hens 10 pounds, this breed was developed in New Jersey during the 1880s. Found in both white and black, the birds can be confused with Australorps except for different leg color and bigger size. The breed shows in the American class for large fowl and the Single Comb Clean Leg class for bantams.

Kraienkoppe: An old Dutch game-type fowl with a small walnut comb, this black-breasted breed comes in red, white, and silver colors but is not part of the *American Standard of Perfection*.

La Fleche: A very striking bird, the breed is distinguished by its large white ear lobes, V-comb, and glowing black plumage. This general-purpose fowl is raised for both eggs and meat and shows in the Continental class

This La Fleche cockerel exhibits the striking V-comb that helps identify this breed. The La Fleche breed was admitted to the *American Standard of Perfection* in 1874. It has white skin and lays white eggs. On average, the cocks weigh 8 pounds and the hens weigh 6.5 pounds. *Kendall Babcock*

for large fowl, while bantams show in the All Other Comb Clean Leg class.

Lakenvelder: Although it has a Dutch name, the breed was developed in Germany. Hens lay white eggs and are non-setters. These birds are quite striking with contrasting colors of a black head and tail with a white body. They show in the Continental class for large fowl and the Single Comb Clean Leg bantam class. A golden version has a rich buff color replacing the white, but is not part of the *American Standard of Perfection* yet.

Lamonas: This bird originated in Maryland from crossbreeding many other breeds, including Leghorns, Rocks, and Dorkings. White is the only standard color. A rare heavy breed that lays white eggs, the large fowl show in the American class and bantams show in the Single Comb Clean Leg class.

Langshan: A long-legged and feather-legged bird, the Langshan comes in black, white, and blue varieties and is faster-maturing than either Brahmas or Cochins that show in the same class of large fowl. The birds don't have the extreme leg feathering of the Cochins, however, making them easier to maintain in a free-range or loose-housing environment. The breed shows in the Asiatic class for large fowl and the Feathered Leg class for bantams.

Leghorn: The breed originated in Italy, but many of its varieties were developed in England and America. There are varieties in both single comb and rose comb, and colors include white, buff, silver, red, cuckoo, mille fleur, mottled light brown, dark brown, and black. Leghorns (especially the whites) are prolific egg-layers, with hens laying as many as three hundred eggs a year. The large fowl show in the Mediterranean class, and the bantams show in the Single Comb or Rose Comb Clean Leg classes, depending on the comb. The unique trait of a lopped single comb in the hen is desired.

Bantam means miniature in the chicken world. Here a bantam white Leghorn cock relaxes with his owner. The bantam's size is ideal for small hands to hold and carry. Handling your chickens daily makes for a very tame and manageable bird regardless of age, breed, or sex. *DeAnn Richards*

Malay: A hard-feathered breed originally bred for fighting, these birds are long-legged with a strawberry comb and are seasonal layers only. They can be quite aggressive toward other birds and humans, so plan plenty of free-range space for this breed. Colors include black, white, spangled, and red pyle, and the wheaten color also shows up but in females only. The breed shows in the All Other Standard Breeds class for large fowl and the All Other Combs Clean Leg class for bantams.

Maran: Birds of the Maran breed are layers of very dark brown eggs, and many feather colors are available, with cuckoo being the most common in the United States. The birds are great for the home flock, but the breed is not in the *American Standard of Perfection* and will not do well at APA-sanctioned shows.

Minorca: These birds come in black, buff, and white. Both the rose and single comb varieties appear in the black and white, but buff is only found in single comb. Since large fowl males can reach 9 pounds and hens 7 ½ pounds, they are the largest and heaviest of the Mediterranean class in large fowl. Bantams are very rare, but they would show in the Single or Rose Comb Clean Leg classes depending on the comb.

53

Modern Game: These birds were developed strictly for exhibition; with their extremely long legs and necks, they are very attractive at shows. Males are required to be dubbed (comb, wattles, and lobes trimmed) for showing, and colors for the breed include black-breasted red, silver duckwing, birchen, brown-red, pyle, lemon blue, blue, black, and white. The breed has its own class (the Modern Game class) in bantams, and large fowls are in the All Other Standard Breeds class.

Nankin Bantam: A true bantam about the size of the Sebrights, the body color of this breed is buff with black main tail feathers, and the comb may be single or rose. These are not included in the *American Standard of Perfection*.

New Hampshire: A dual-purpose breed developed in New Hampshire, these birds mature early and lay large brown eggs. An American classic for the backyard flock keeper, this large fowl shows in the American class, and bantams show in the Single Comb Clean Leg class.

Norwegian Jaerhon: The only truly Norwegian breed, these are active and hardy birds that lay large white eggs. Day-old chicks can be sexed by color, and the breed is not included in the *American Standard of Perfection*.

Old English Game: Colors for this breed include black-breasted red, crele, silver duckwing, spangled, golden duckwing, and lemon blue. The Old English Game breed has its own class in the bantam size, even though the birds look like they would belong in the Single Comb Clean Leg class. Cocks must be dubbed (comb, wattles, and lobes trimmed) for showing, and large fowl are very rare but would show in the All Other Standard Breeds class.

Orpington: A great all-around bird for the beginner, Orpingtons have very mellow personalities and make great pets. Developed as a dual-purpose breed, these birds make a decent-sized carcass for table fowl and are excellent winter layers of large brown eggs. Buff, black, white, and blue are recognized colors, and large fowl show in the English class while bantams show in the Single Comb Clean Leg class.

Penedescenca (Black): A very rare breed, these birds have an unusual comb that is single-like in the front and crown-like in the rear. They have a temperament like the Leghorn but produce a very dark brown egg. The breed is not found in the *American Standard of Perfection*.

Phoenix: Descendants of the chickens seen in Japanese illustrations that have tails fifteen to twenty feet or longer, the modern-day Phoenix males, however, seldom get tails longer than a few feet and require great care to do so. The hens are great mothers but are only seasonal layers. Colors include silver and golden, and the breed shows in the All Other Standard Breeds large fowl class and in the Single Comb Clean Leg class for the bantams.

Plymouth Rock: The most common of the dual-purpose breeds found in today's backyard flocks, the Plymouth Rock is an American classic that comes in many colors, including white, buff, black, and the very popular barred. The partridge variety features a dark-brown penciled pattern on the females with the males a showy tri-color of red, brown, and black. All varieties lay brown eggs and show in the American class for large fowl and the Single Comb Clean Leg class for bantams.

Polish: Also known as the "top hat" breed, the Polish is the most popular of the crested breeds. An ornamental, non-setting breed that lays a white egg, its most prominent features are the feathered crest on the head and the small V-comb. The birds appear in many colors in both bearded and non-bearded versions, including white-crested black,

The extreme crest of feathers on Polish chickens gives them a limited sight range, especially in the males. This trait can make birds of this breed easier targets for birds of prey, which is one factor you must consider before buying these beautiful birds. *Kendall Babcock*

black-crested white, white, silver, and buff-laced. You can purchase bearded or non-bearded chicks—the rest have been commercially bred together and will not make good show stock. Large fowl show in the Continental class, with bantams showing in the All Other Comb Clean Leg class.

Redcap: A huge comb covered by spikes gives the breed its name, and it is very unique, but the comb is hard to maintain in colder climates. Large fowl show in the English class, and bantams show as All Other Comb Clean Leg.

Rhode Island: A great layer of brown eggs, the Rhode Island is best known for the single-comb red variety, though it also comes as a rose-comb red and a rose-comb white. When it was developed in Rhode Island in the 1830s, various breeds were used in its genetic makeup. The desired red color is a deep, rich mahogany; the rusty red seen in commercial varieties is not desirable for show stock. Depending on the comb, all varieties show in the American class as large fowl and the Single Comb or Rose Comb Clean Leg classes as bantams.

Rosecomb Bantam: A true bantam, this breed comes in a wide variety of colors, with standards of black, blue, and white. The birds have a distinct, large white earlobe and a diminutive size, and they show in the Rose Comb Clean Leg class.

The rose comb of this Rhode Island white cockerel is unique because its many points end in a spike. The comb's overall smaller size and closeness to the chicken's skull help keep it from becoming frostbitten during cold weather. *Kendall Babcock*

These gangly ten-week-old chicks are spangled Russian Orloffs. This breed is quite rare in the United States but is stocked by a few hatcheries. They are easily identified by their hawk-like head profile and unique color pattern, even at this young age. *Kelly Damaschke*

Russian Orloff: A large, gamey-looking fowl, the Russian Orloff is a rare breed in the United States. Its unique characteristics are a round head with full muffs and a beard topped off by a small raspberry comb. Hens lay a light brown egg but are known to be poor layers. The birds are very hardy and resistant to harsh winter weather, and feather colors include spangled and cuckoo. The breed is not found in the *American Standard of Perfection*.

Sebright Bantam: Very attractive little birds found only as bantams, the breed's recognized colors are silver (white with black lacing) and gold (golden buff with black lacing), and it shows in the Rose Comb Clean Leg class. A cock should weigh only 26 ounces and a hen only 22 ounces. The Sebright has a rose comb, and the males must be hen-feathered, which is a disqualification in other breeds.

Serama: This is a very tiny breed: desired birds weigh less than 15 ounces, with under 12 ounces preferred for both sexes. Relatively new to America, the Serama is not in the *American Standard of Perfection*.

Shamo: The Shamo is a hard-feathered game breed that was developed for use as a fighting fowl. The feathering is exceedingly short and hard, to the extent that the breastbone is left bare. Colors listed in the *American Standard of Perfection* include black, black-breasted red, and dark. The breed is very territorial and aggressive toward other birds, so give each bird plenty of space. Large fowl show in the All Other Standard Breeds class and bantams in the All Other Comb Clean Leg class.

Sicilian Buttercup: This rare breed originated in Sicily, and the birds have a unique cup-shaped comb with many points on the outside edges. Also, males have a different color pattern than the females. The Buttercup is part of the Mediterranean class in large fowl and the All Other Comb Clean Leg class in bantams.

Silkie: Truly a unique breed from the Orient, these birds are known for their barbless feathers that give an overall fluffy appearance. They have black skin and bones, a fifth toe, and a mulberry-colored walnut comb and appear in both bearded and non-bearded varieties. You should purchase chicks that are sold by bearded or non-bearded classifications, since the rest have been commercially bred together and will not make good show stock. Colors include black, blue, buff, partridge, and white. Silkie hens are among the best mothers to hatch eggs, and the breed is a true bantam (there is no large fowl counterpart) that shows in the Feathered Leg class.

Spitzhauben: The word *spitzhauben* means "pointed hat or bonnet." The national breed of Switzerland, this is a small-crested breed with a V-comb and spangled-type coloration. Hens lay a white egg, and the birds are easier to keep than the larger-crested Polish, though they are not in the *American Standard of Perfection.*

Sultan: This breed has a full crest, muff, and beard; heavily feathered shanks with vulture hocks (a disqualification in most breeds); five toes; and a small, V-shaped comb. Large fowl show in the All Other Standard Breeds class, and bantams show in the Feathered Leg class. The standard color is white.

Sumatra: Regal and decorative fowl originating from the Indonesian island of Sumatra, this breed's accepted colors are white, blue, and (most commonly) black. The birds sport beautiful, lustrous black plumage, shining with an intense, beetle-green sheen. Also, cocks frequently have a cluster of several spurs on each leg (a breed peculiarity). Both sexes have a long tail carried low, though the males have a particularly impressive heavy sweep of long, curving, sharply pointed tail feathers. Large fowl show in the Any Other class, and bantams show in the All Other Comb Clean Leg class.

Sussex: An English heavy breed that has been around for over a hundred years, the feather colors of the Sussex include speckled, red, and light, and the birds feature a single comb. The large fowl bird makes a good table fowl, since the cocks should weigh in at nine pounds and the hens at seven pounds. Hens are fair setters and lay a light brown egg. Large fowl show in the English class and bantams in the Single Comb Clean Leg class.

Turkens (Naked Neck): The name for these birds comes from their odd appearance, like a turkey, with so many feathers missing on the neck and breast. This breed was intended to be a fowl for easier plucking, since it has less than half the number of feathers of other breeds of the same size. It is also very tolerant to heat due to fewer feathers. Red, white, buff, and black colors are standard, and these are easy-going birds, decent layers, and still quite hardy in cold weather. Large fowl show in the All Other Standard Breeds class, and bantams show in the Single Comb Clean Leg class.

Vorwerk: A German breed developed as a good layer, the Vorwerk is also a fair-sized meat producer, as well as an easy keeper. Plumage for this breed is reminiscent of a Lakenvelder, with the white replaced by a dark buff. This breed does not appear in the *American Standard of Perfection.*

Welsummer: A Dutch breed that takes its name from the small village of Welsum, the Welsummer was developed just after the turn of the twentieth century. Its main characteristic is its large dark-brown egg. These birds are good free-range foragers, and coloring in both sexes is similar to that of the light-brown Leghorns. Large fowl show in the Continental class, and bantams show in the Single Comb Clean Leg class.

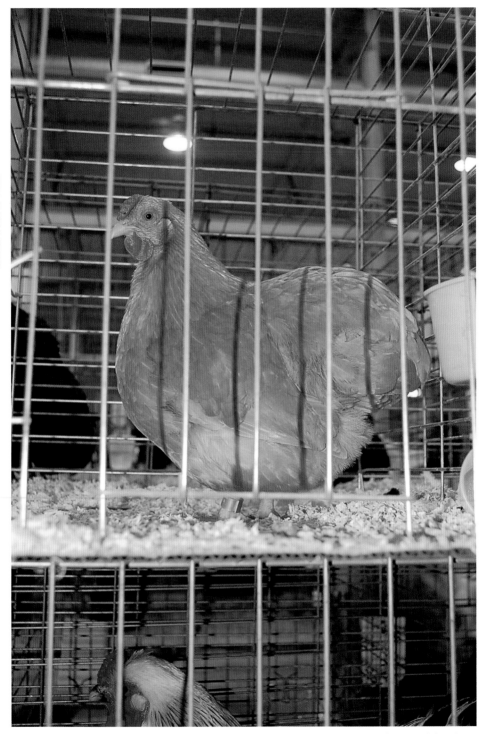

This gentle, large fowl, buff Wyandotte hen is well prepared for show day. She has been kept out of direct sunlight to keep her rich color from fading, her feathers are in great condition, her comb and wattles are a rich red, and she is used to the cage area and is standing well. *Corallina Breuer*

White-Faced Black Spanish: A slow-maturing, non-setting bird that produces large, chalky-white eggs, the breed's distinguishing features are a white face and large, low-hanging, white earlobes. This is probably the oldest breed of the large fowl Mediterranean class, though it is quite rare today. Bantams show in the Single Comb Clean Leg class.

Wyandotte: This is a popular American breed for backyard flocks and the show enthusiast. Varieties accepted in the *American Standard of Perfection* are the golden-laced, white, black, buff, Columbian, partridge, silver-laced, and silver-penciled. Large fowl of this breed are great layers of good-sized brown eggs and reach a weight of

This buff Wyandotte chick's rose comb is identifiable already at one day old. The egg tooth that the chick uses to break out of the shell is still attached to its beak, but it will fall off in another day or two. *DeAnn Richards*

The American Livestock Breeds Conservancy lists the following chicken breeds as "threatened": Ancona, Cubalaya, Dorking, Java, Lakenvelder, Langshan, and Sussex.

Threatened status means that there are fewer than one thousand breeding birds in the United States, with seven or fewer primary breeding flocks, and also that the breed is globally endangered.

8 1/2 pounds for the males. Calm, peaceable birds that adapt well to most situations, the large fowl show in the American class, and the bantams show in the Rose Comb Clean Leg class. Wyandottes usually contribute to some of the largest bantam classes at shows sanctioned by the ABA and APA.

Yokohama: This is a breed of long-tail birds with pea combs. A non-molting gene allows the male's tail feathers to grow very long, but extra care and a lot of patience are necessary if you are planning to raise or exhibit this breed. Colors listed in the *American Standard of Perfection* are white and red shoulder.

Still having trouble deciding on a breed or breeds? If you have enough room, why not order twenty-five chicks from a hatchery assortment in either straight-run or pullets-only? You will get an economical start to many breeds and can learn about the unique traits firsthand as you watch that first batch grow. Plan to ask another poultry enthusiast for help in identifying the growing birds if you still are uncertain after reviewing the breed list and chick identification sections.

The breed of a purebred chick can be identified using several clues, such as the number of toes, comb style, and fluff on its shanks. This group of ten-week-old chicks includes black Leghorns, black Javas, white-faced black Spanish, and a black Crevecoeur. *Tara Kindschi*

Chick Identification

If you ordered multiple breeds of birds or if you ordered the hatchery special, you may be having trouble identifying which chicks are which breed. Refer to the Complete Breed List for any special features that exist even in a day-old chick. Clues to identify breeds include the following:

- Are there extra toes? Breeds like Silkies, Dorkings, and Sultans will have this even at hatch.
- Are there feathers on the legs and/ or inner and outer toes? A Langshan only has feathers on the outer toe and shank, while a Cochin would also have feathering fluff on the inner toe.
- Can you see the start of a crest? The "topknot" is part of the skull and shows up early in breeds like the Polish, Crevecoeurs, Sultans, Houdans, and Silkies.
- What color is the skin? Silkies have black skin.
- What is the comb style? You can tell the difference between a single and rose comb in a day-old chick, even though the comb is tiny. Look carefully to determine the difference between Rocks, Wyandottes, and the like. The distinctive

"horn" on the comb of the La Fleche is small but visible.

- What color are the legs? A fluffy light-gray to white chick with black legs is probably a white Jersey Giant instead of a white Rock.
- What about first feathers? First feathers can be misleading. An adult solid-black bird may have been a black/white mix as a chick in down and its first three wing feathers may be pure white. Keep watching, and the next few wing feathers and tail feathers may be a better clue as to what breed it is.
- Do you think you have all one variety but the chicks are different colors? Some hybrids may be sex-linked in coloring, meaning that the males (even as day-old chicks) are a different color than the females.
- Did you order salmon Faverolles and the chicks are all yellow? Within two weeks, the feathers will come in much darker on the males and a lighter salmon color on the females.
- Are some of your blue chicks black? When mating for blue coloring, a percentage of birds will always come out black-and-splash in color. Be patient to see what great shades you will see.

This black Jersey Giant chick shows the single comb of its breed. It is quite common for solid black breeds of chickens to have chicks that are partly black and white. Even the first few wing feathers that emerge may be white. *DeAnn Richards*

Silver Campine chicks have some of the cutest markings. Many breeds of chicks exhibit striped markings that turn into a variety of beautiful feather patterns as they mature. *Tara Kindschi*

Different breeds feather-in at different rates. This seven-day-old partridge Cochin doesn't have any wing feathers. Black Leghorn chicks of the same age will have more than a dozen feathers in on each wing. *Kendall Babcock*

HATCHING AND RAISING CHICKS

Natural Incubation

Chicks can be raised in two ways. The first is natural incubation, where fertile eggs are put under a broody hen who keeps the eggs warm under her body for twenty-one days. She partially rolls the eggs every day to keep the growing embryos from sticking to the inside shells. At hatching, her body keeps the chicks warm and protected. The chicks begin exploring for food in a day or two after their legs become stable and they are a little stronger.

A juvenile black Cochin enjoys the sunshine on a warm spring day. Birds this size need careful protection from a wide variety of predators including cats, dogs, hawks, and aggressive adult chickens. The early comb coloring indicates this may be a cockerel, but it cannot be positively identified yet. *Corallina Breuer*

This hen had a successful hatch and is calm enough to allow the photographer to get in close for a picture. The mothering instincts of many broody hens cause them to be very protective of their young and therefore aggressive to humans. Use caution when near a broody hen. *Kelly Damaschke*

It's a great experience to watch tiny little fluff balls turn into full-fledged adult chickens in just months. You can incubate eggs or let your hens raise their own chicks to increase your flock. With careful timing of egg collection and broody hens, you can make use of the natural process for your flock replacements, additions, or sales.

This chick has pipped out a complete opening and is ready to push its way out of the shell after a brief rest. This chick/egg was removed from the incubator for illustration purposes only. Don't disturb hatching eggs for any reason. *Kelly Damaschke*

If a hen is left unattended and allowed to roam free, she will sometimes lay her eggs in one spot every day for a week or two until she has six to twenty eggs, which is called a clutch. The brooding and setting occurs most often in spring when the hen's natural mothering and reproduction instincts take over. This is the same way most wild birds, including wild ducks and geese, raise their young. No human intervention is involved.

The humans who first domesticated chickens watched this natural phenomenon and took extra steps with their own flocks to create more and diverse offspring. They discovered that a hen didn't care if the eggs under her were actually hers or were laid by another hen. This trick still works today.

With careful timing of egg collection and broody hens, you can make use of the natural process for your flock replacements, additions, or sales. Here are some tips for having a successful hatching project.

Fertile Eggs

To produce offspring, you must have a male mating with the females whose eggs you are collecting. Use the same variety of chicken for both parents for purebred offspring. Hens must be with that rooster for at least two weeks before the eggs are considered pure. Using a mix of breeds will result in crossbred offspring. A hen can sit on six to eighteen eggs, depending on her body size and the size of the eggs.

Artificial insemination may be needed if you are trying to raise a rumpless or heavily feathered breed and are having zero or very low fertility rates. The insemination process involves using a kitchen-variety baster to collect semen manually from the male bird and place it into the cloaca (or the reproductive opening) of the hen. The process needs to be repeated after a hen lays three to four eggs. Consult a breeder who has successfully used this process before attempting it on your own birds.

Egg Collection and Storage

Eggs can be stored for up to two weeks in a cool, dark location. The ideal temperature is sixty degrees Fahrenheit. A ten-degree range within that temperature is fine. Don't store the eggs in the refrigerator. Only wash eggs that are very dirty. Turn the stored eggs from pointed end up to pointed end down and vice versa daily.

Broody Hens

Spring is the best time to try to have a hen raise chicks. Some hens can be lured into setting by placing them in a semi-dark, quiet, deeply bedded cage away from the flock. It becomes clear that your hens are broody when you have to remove them constantly from the nest boxes while collecting eggs. Some breeds are much more likely to be setters than other breeds. Good broody hens include Silkies and Cochin bantams. Avoid Leghorns, Anconas, and Andalusians for broody hens.

Location

The broody hen is best kept in a separate cage with her own feed and water supply. She will drink and eat very little during the incubation time and will often only come off her nest of eggs once a day for less than fifteen minutes.

Rearing

The chicks stay with the hen after they have hatched. She helps them find feed and is their heat source until they are fully feathered and start roosting next to her instead of under her. The hen and her chicks are best raised in a separate area, since other birds will often be aggressive toward the young chicks.

A large fowl buff Orpington hen shows her desire to brood by sitting all day in a nesting box. Broody hens, whether they have a real clutch of eggs or not, don't care to leave the nest and may peck when you try to move them or reach underneath for their eggs. *Shelly Sonsalla*

Incubators use controlled heat and humidity sources to replicate closely a hen's body warmth.

This jumble of barred feathering is a broody hen and her almost fully feathered chicks. Hen-raised chicks will continue to seek warmth and protection under a hen's wings for several months and will even try to roost under her wings when older. *DeAnn Richards*

Artificial Incubation

Collecting and storing fertile eggs produces the same results as natural incubation, but you use an incubator instead of a broody hen. Incubators were invented by chicken keepers who wanted to have more control of their flock's hatches by setting larger numbers of eggs than a hen could raise. Also, they did not want to be limited by the number of broody hens available, and many of the breeds being developed had lost their natural broody instincts.

Incubators use controlled heat and humidity sources to replicate closely a hen's body warmth. The most economical and common incubators are box-types made of a polystyrene foam product that hold about three dozen large fowl eggs and more for bantam-size eggs. This style of incubator

This large-capacity older incubator has a window for viewing the hatching process without disturbing the heat or humidity settings. Each row of trays is set with eggs from a different breed. The five-hundred-egg capacity of this incubator is much larger than you will need for backyard flock use. *Tara Kindschi*

65

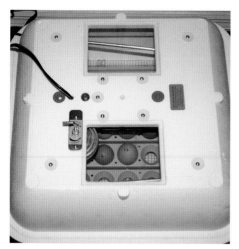

Many tabletop incubators are made of a polystyrene foam product and come with a heat element and built-in water trays. This particular model includes an egg turner to cut down on daily labor. Any incubator you purchase will come with extensive instructions for use depending on the type of eggs you will be incubating. *DeAnn Richards*

comes in still-air or forced-air models that run at slightly different temperatures. Other more complex and larger-capacity incubators are also available and should be researched carefully to determine your needs before purchasing. Any incubator you purchase should include directions for use.

Eggs being incubated must be turned or rolled halfway around at least twice a day. This is something that the hen automatically does while she is setting. You will need to half-roll the eggs at least twice every day or install an automatic egg turner in your incubator. To keep track of eggs being turned, mark each egg with an "X" on one side and an "O" on the other side. Stop turning the eggs at day nineteen of the incubation process to give the chicks a chance to turn themselves inside and start breaking out of the shell.

Candling is a method to check if an embryo is developing in the incubating eggs. Candling is best done at day five of the incubation process. Commercial candlers can be purchased, but you can also use a hand-held, high-powered flashlight. Here's how you candle an egg:

Start with a completely dark room. Hold one of the incubating eggs in your right hand and the flashlight in your left. Turn the flashlight on and cup the lens with your forefinger and thumb forming a small circle. Practice making the circle larger and smaller by opening and closing your fingers. Make a circle the size of a quarter, hold the large end

A simple polystyrene foam incubator equipped with an egg turner can hold forty-two large fowl eggs. The variety of eggshell colors shows the multiple breeds being incubated at once. This is a nice size and price range of incubator for the home flock keeper. Larger, more elaborate and expensive incubators can be purchased as needs expand. *Corallina Breuer*

This broody hen allows a picture to be taken of an egg from her clutch that is pipped. Note the already hatched, completely dry chick tucked under the hen for warmth. The absorbed yolk provides a chick with enough nutrients for several days. *Kelly Damaschke*

of the egg over the circle, and form a tight seal with your fingers. You should see a red spot with veins coming off it like a large spider if an embryo has started to grow. If you see a clear glow, the egg was not fertile, and no chick will develop. You may have trouble seeing through the shell in a green or very dark brown egg. If you repeat this process a week later, you should see a much larger embryo and a heartbeat/pulsation. Discard all the eggs that were clear. This saves space in the incubator and time turning eggs that won't hatch.

The hatching process from when a chick pips an egg (makes a hole from the inside through the egg) until the chick breaks completely out may take twelve to thirty-six hours. Do not rush the process or open the incubator. The first chicks that hatch can run around inside the incubator for one to two days until the rest of the batch catches up. Let all chicks dry completely before moving them to a brooder or container.

Raising Chicks

A successful twenty-one-day incubation process results in fluffy, peeping chicks that are prepared for life. Just before hatching, the chick absorbs into its abdomen the remaining yolk part of the egg. This supplies the chick with a food source for its first days of life.

Notice the puffy cheeks on this black chick. The clean leg, lack of a crest, and comb type identify this chick as being a black Ameraucana. It is common for all black breeds to be partially white as chicks, especially on the underbody and breast areas. *Kendall Babcock*

67

Spreading the wing of this week-old golden-penciled Hamburg shows how the first feathers are a simple version of the complex color pattern that the mature feathers will have. A chicken grows three sets of feathers before it shows its final adult plumage. *Tara Kindschi*

always cup your other hand over its back to keep it from jumping and falling to the ground. Children under three to four years of age seldom know what grip is too hard and will need an adult to supervise any chick-holding.

Juvenile Care

Depending on outside weather conditions, a heat source is no longer needed and constant lighting can be weaned off the birds by five to eight weeks of age. By this time, the chicks have grown a full set of feathers and are trying to fly and jump up. It is time to introduce them to more space and roosts. The chicks will probably be sleeping away from the heat, which is a clue that it is no longer needed.

The new area should be bigger, with a space of one square foot per large fowl bird. It should also have enough height inside so birds can fly onto roosts at night. The first roost should be made of wood. Straight branches or dowels work well for roosts. Hang them or raise them off the ground four to eight inches. Because you won't be lighting the coop for twenty-four hours a day, the young birds will want to sleep when it gets dark. Their natural instinct is to get off the ground and up and away from predators. Switching feed from starter to grower can be done at this time, but staying on starter is also acceptable.

A larger brooder setup can easily be made out of scrap wood and can house either larger numbers of chicks or growing birds. This homemade covered box is in use for a broody hen and her young chicks. The bulbs are for light and not heat. *DeAnn Richards*

A growing bird's space requirements increase both horizontally and vertically. These juvenile gold-laced Polish are rubbing and damaging their crest feathers as they go in and out of their brooder setup. *Jerilyn Johnson*

This mixed flock of growing pullets enjoys a temporary yard made of chicken wire and posts that can be moved as the birds eat the grass and dirty the ground. This kind of setup requires a careful lookout for birds of prey that can easily attack this size of chicken from the sky. Note the barred Plymouth Rock in front and the red Turken in the middle. *Kelly Damaschke*

This is a good time to start combining different ages using the following methods:

- Introduce the chicks to your flock when they are the same size as the rest of your flock.
- Make sure there is enough room for all the chicks. Overcrowding stresses birds.
- Make hiding places by setting up a few boxes, or make a shelter with branches.
- Move everyone to the new pen at once so no one feels dominant. Neither group will have established ownership, and everyone will be on equal, unfamiliar footing.

You may also want to separate any excess roosters or other birds you don't plan to keep and sell or butcher them.

Continue raising and enjoying your birds and gradually increase the roost height and feeder height to that of adult birds. Depending on breed, lighting, and growth rate, you can expect your pullets to start laying eggs at five to eight months of age. At this same age, cockerels will turn their earlier crowing attempts into a full-fledged wake-up call.

Several large cardboard boxes can be combined to form a large area for chick brooding in a garage. The plank across the top keeps the heat bulb and its cords securely away for fire safety. The high sides and folded top prevent heat from escaping when the chicks are younger and will help control flying and roosting as they get older. *DeAnn Richards*

A newly hatched partridge Rock large fowl chick waits for the rest of the clutch to hatch. The pipping (breaking the shell) and hatching process can take a clutch one to three days to complete. Leaving the hatched chicks in the incubator while the other chicks catch up is beneficial, since the hatched chicks can strengthen their legs and dry off. *DeAnn Richards*

ADULT BIRD BASICS

A small flock of laying hens will supply a family with great-tasting eggs year-round when adequate feed, shelter, and lighting are provided. Laying hens require twelve to sixteen hours of light per day. Short winter days mean you must use a combination of sunlight and electric lights to achieve the amount of light required. *Kris Even*

IN THIS SECTION

All of the pleasures of raising chicks and juveniles can be experienced with adult birds. Observe your chickens as they busily get ready to roost. Listen to their purr-like sounds as they settle down for a night's rest. Enjoy their enthusiasm when they burst forth to the outdoors as you open the coop at daybreak. You'll soon recognize the scolding hen that doesn't want to get off her eggs and the most prideful rooster that constantly struts around his flock. Chickens in a flock have different personalities, temperaments, routines, and preferences. They may ignore you or remember that you are a source of treats at certain times of the day and come running when they see you. Some chickens may be favorite show birds or produce colored eggs that you arrange artfully in a carton to sell to neighbors. Your chicken flock can be a source of constant entertainment for both you and your family.

Raising and caring for chickens on a daily basis is a great learning experience for young adults. Birds that are handled daily become tame and friendly. Many flock keepers consider their birds to be pets and not just livestock. Poultry keeping is a great hobby for the whole family. *Kelly Damaschke*

To get the maximum amount of joy from your flock, you and your family need to provide your birds with adequate care to keep them healthy and happy. Raising adult birds does require some basic starting supplies and special knowledge about care and management of the flock.

Waterers

Purchase waterers from farm supply stores. Many designs and sizes are suitable for your coop. Disinfect waterers on a regular basis; it must happen weekly during the summer.

The waterer should hold enough water for two days. Place it off of the ground for cleanliness and ease of drinking. A domed top keeps chickens from perching on top of the waterer and keeps their droppings out of the water supply. Use a heated base during cold weather to keep the water from freezing. Automatic watering systems run from a hose and low-pressure valve. They are a great time-saver but only work when the outside temperatures are above freezing. Automatic watering systems must also be cleaned weekly.

Feeders

Several types of feeders can be used for adult birds. All are designed to keep the feed from being wasted and the birds and their droppings out of the food source. You will need separate spaces for feed, grit, and oyster shell. Allow enough room at feeders for all chickens to be able to eat at the same time. Cylinder-type metal or plastic feeders can be hung from the coop ceiling at the height appropriate for your birds. Trough-type feeders are often raised off the ground. They should have a rod or wire cover to keep the chickens from hopping entirely into the trough. Feeders can also be built of wood.

A galvanized metal feeder can be hung from the ceiling of a chicken coop and raised or lowered to the correct height for the flock. Weekly cleaning will keep the feeder free of droppings and dust. *Kendall Babcock*

This round plastic feeder holds several pounds of feed and is hung a few inches off the ground for this large fowl flock. It is protected from the elements by a metal roof and is filled daily and cleaned weekly. *Shelly Sonsalla*

Roosts

Have a minimum of eight to ten inches of roost available per large fowl bird and six to eight inches of roost per bird for bantam breeds. A series of stacking bars rising from six inches to five feet with the lowest bar being the farthest from the wall and each bar getting closer to the wall like stair steps makes the best use of space for a large flock. Metal and plastic tend to be too slippery for the chickens to grip comfortably. The area directly under the roosts will accumulate the most droppings, so create a heavier bed there, and keep feeders and waterers out from under this area.

Nesting Boxes

You should have one nesting box for every four to six hens. Boxes can be built using plywood or purchased as metal or plastic boxes. The types that hang on the wall are best, since they won't take up valuable floor space. Boxes should be placed on the west or east wall in a south-facing coop to keep the hens out of the hot afternoon sun. Disinfecting and cleaning is easier with the metal or plastic nests, but their cost may be prohibitive to the small-flock owner. Nest boxes should have a bar attached to the front to help the hens get in and out of the boxes without breaking eggs.

Nest boxes should be bedded with straw, shavings, sawdust, or shredded paper to prevent egg breakage when hens enter or leave the nests. Broken eggs can encourage an egg-eating habit. Once that bad habit starts, a hen may start to break eggs on purpose to eat them. Other birds may follow suit, and soon you have a whole flock of egg-eating hens. The habit is impossible to break, so care must be used to prevent it from starting. Collecting eggs twice a day will also help avoid egg breakage.

Feed

Chickens require a healthy, well-balanced diet. For adult birds, this is easily obtained through the use of pre-formulated feeds much like they

If your hens aren't laying eggs in the nest but seem to prefer the ground, try putting deeper bedding in the nest and adding a wooden egg or golf ball to mimic a real egg. This sometimes helps hens get the idea to lay their eggs in the nest box.

have eaten since they were chicks. This feed is generally available in fifty-pound bags at local feed or pet stores. There are different formulas for different ages and types of birds, including the following three basic chicken feeds:

- Starter for one day to eight weeks of age; a fine crumble-type feed.
- Grower for birds eight weeks to egg-laying age and for meat birds.
- Layer for adult birds that have started egg production; available as a small crumble or large crumble.
- Mash for egg-layers is a powder-type feed that can be ground at local feed mills.

Many companies carry basic feeds. Some also have special formulas that include all-vegetarian, show feeds with higher oils, scratch feeds to be used as a treat, and concentrates to be mixed with your own grains to form a balanced feed.

Eggs laid in nests without bedding have a tendency to break. Hens scratch and draw bedding out every time they enter a nest. Clean out soiled bedding and add new bedding in the form of straw, shavings, or shredded paper as a part of your weekly chore schedule. *Kendall Babcock*

Pre-formulated complete feeds are the best choice for the backyard flock. There are many feed companies and formulas, such as organic, show, layer, starter, and grower feeds. Plan to purchase only as much as you will use in two to three weeks and store in a clean, dry area away from bird droppings, rodents, and temperature extremes. *Tara Kindschi*

Formulas or recipes for custom-mixed feed are available through your local county agricultural extension office or feed cooperative. The batch size that most feed stores or mills will make is too large for backyard flock use, and the feed can spoil or lose nutritional value if not used right away.

Feed should be offered free-choice, except when raising broiler-type meat birds. Free-choice means to have the food always in the feeder for the birds to eat as often and as much as they like.

It is important to keep your feed supply fresh, dry, and free of droppings from

> Did you know chickens don't have teeth? They swallow their food whole. The crop, an enlarged part of the gullet for temporary food storage, uses small stones called grit to grind food before it enters the digestive system.

> Chicken-catching can be a time-consuming chore if you have any wild breeds or your chickens are free-range. Several tools are available to help with this chore. A fish net or a net made for avian and bird-catching (with or without a telescoping handle) comes in handy at home or shows. There is also an old-fashioned simple tool called a "chicken catcher" made with a wood handle and a sturdy wire extension that has a hook on the end and is designed to grab a walking bird by one or both feet.

birds and rodents, such as mice and rats. Unfortunately, rodents love chicken coops for the warmth, feed, and feathers for nests. Keep the feed in a sealed container or away from the main coop to prevent access by rodents and to maintain the nutritional value. Try to purchase and store only a week's worth of feed. Old feed, especially in opened bags, can quickly lose its nutrient quality.

Grit

Grit needs to be a part of every chicken's diet. Grit consists of the small stones that a chicken ingests to help its crop grind feed. A constant supply of grit is needed and should be offered free-choice. Start introducing very small grit to chicks at two to three weeks of age by sprinkling a small amount on top of their feed. This tiny grit can be purchased in the caged-bird section at a pet store and comes in small ½- to 1-pound boxes labeled for cockatiels, parrots, and similar caged birds. This amount is perfect for providing twenty-five chicks with grit for several weeks until they move up to the small to medium grit that is available at local feed stores in 20- to 30-pound bags. Plan to share this size of a bag with a fellow poultry enthusiast or store it carefully, since it will keep and last a long time. Chickens

This feeder has legs to raise the trough off the floor to a comfortable height for chickens. It also features a division on each end for grit or oyster shell. A wire cover allows the chickens to eat but keeps them from jumping in. *Kendall Babcock*

that free-range exclusively may find their own small stones while foraging, but always have grit available in case they don't.

Oyster Shell

Another item that needs to be a part of every laying hen's diet is extra calcium, used to help form strong eggshells. This extra calcium is easily supplied in the form of broken oyster shells, which come in twenty- to thirty-pound bags through a local feed store. Oyster shell should be offered free-choice after pullets start laying.

Treats/Scratch Feed

Chickens love treats in the form of table scraps, grass clippings, weeds from gardens and flowerbeds, whole grains, sunflower seeds, and more! Treats should not be used to replace balanced feed that is available free-choice, but balanced-feed consumption may go down considerably on a day when there are a lot of scraps and weeds given. That is great savings for the pocketbook. Use care and avoid feeding meat scraps and rotten food that may contain harmful bacteria.

Bedding

Bedding materials include hay or straw, wood shavings, sawdust, and shredded paper. Bedding must be dry and absorbent. Shavings and shredded paper are both very absorbent, but hay or straw is sometimes a more cost-effective alternative. Seeds contained in hay and straw are loved by the birds and promote scratching and turning of the bedding. A thickness of three to six inches is recommended for shavings and shredded paper, with six to eight inches for hay or straw bedding.

Once bedding becomes damp or filled with droppings, it must be replaced with fresh bedding. How often it needs to be replaced varies based on number and size of birds, type and thickness of bedding, and weather conditions.

The deep-litter method is a form of in-coop composting with your bedding of choice. It is a very popular solution for avid gardeners, since it supplies them with ready-to-use compost. This method involves a very deep bedding of eight to twelve inches of organic material that is often a mix of hay, straw, shavings, shredded paper, mulch, and dead leaves. The idea is to have the hens do the turning and composting work associated with a standard compost pile. Scratch feed is sprinkled in the litter daily to force the hens to dig and turn the litter to find the treats. Lawn clippings, garden waste, and the like are added to the mix. The important factor is that there is no spoilage due to excess moisture. When compost is needed for gardens or flowerbeds, all you need to do is remove a portion of the litter from the coop.

Egg Supplies

Supplies that are needed for laying hens include the following:

- **Cartons:**
  These can be reused from previous grocery store purchases or purchased from poultry supply houses.
- **Gathering basket:**
  The old-fashioned-style basket made of wire works best to keep eggs from rolling and cracking or breaking.
- **Washing equipment:**
  Commercial egg-washers are available, but you may find a sink, dish soap, and washcloth are adequate for home use. Check state and local regulations to determine the best egg-washing process if you plan to sell eggs.
- **Egg scale:**
  Used to grade eggs by size. This is not mandatory, but it's a good way to determine what size eggs your hens lay. If you plan to sell eggs, check out state regulations concerning grading and labeling.

Confining Birds

Although you may choose to allow your flock to free-range or let your chickens into a yard daily, there are still times when the birds must remain in the coop. It is times like these that you must recheck your bird-numbers-to-square-foot ratio. Reasons to keep your birds in all day include the following:

- Extreme weather:
  Keep your chickens inside during very cold weather, pouring rain, or deep snow.
- Vacation:
  Be sure birds are safe when you are away for an extended time. It's also easier for a temporary caregiver to attend to the birds in your flock if they are confined.
- Observation/Catching:
  It's easier to catch birds for washing, blood testing, taking to a show, or giving medications when they are confined.
- Predator protection:
  Prevent daytime hits by a predator. Keep the flock safe until a predator problem can be dealt with.

Adding Adult Birds

Plan ahead before making an impulse purchase at a show or swap. Your new birds need to be quarantined to keep your existing flock safe and healthy from any diseases or bad habits the new birds may have. There are simple steps to follow to quarantine the new birds. Have a place for the new birds to live away from your current flock for an extended period of time. They need to be kept away from your other birds for at least thirty days. You will need to build a pen or have a large cage in a building separate from your current flock. Don't share feeders or waterers between your flock and the newcomers without first disinfecting both carefully. Visit your existing flock first, and then go to the newcomers. This will help limit the spread of germs and bacteria only toward the newcomers and not to your existing flock.

Observe the new birds carefully. Look for any signs of illness or disease. Also look for bad habits, such as egg-eating. When handling these birds, look carefully for mites and lice. Always wash your hands after handling your new birds.

Start the newcomers on the feed program you currently use and watch to see that they are eating and drinking well. Your water may taste different to them, and your feed may be a different mix, so they may not want to eat or drink in their new surroundings.

If at any time the birds appear less than healthy in those thirty days, treat the birds as the signs indicate and separate them until you have thirty days of completely healthy birds. Some diseases may not show up right away, so be patient with your quarantine, and the result will be a better introduction of new birds into your existing flock.

A chicken or small-animal swap is usually a one-day or a morning sale hosted by a poultry club or other group. Swaps are often held at fairgrounds, and you will see ads for them at the local feed store or in the *Poultry Press*, or you'll hear about them from other poultry enthusiasts. They tend to start early in the morning and are done by noon. Get there early for the best finds. You can also attend in the hopes of trading chickens. You'll more than likely see people buying and selling birds, other small animals, and supplies. Use caution when purchasing at a show or swap. Not all sellers are scrupulous and follow quarantine procedures with any purchase. And remember to check state and local regulations for specific rules on poultry sales.

Pecking Order

In any flock of chickens, each chicken's personality comes into play in the order of dominance. There's a dominant bird, usually male and aggressive, all the way down the scale to a meek and gentle lowest bird. Older chickens will generally dominate over younger chickens.

The dominance order is established by pecking, chasing, fighting, bumping chests, and so on. If chicks grow up together, they have worked out dominance by a few weeks of age, and therefore peace within the flock is generally set. But if you introduce a new bird or birds to the flock, everyone must rework it all out, from the dominant down to the lowest. It may only take a few hours, or it may take a week or more. It is the natural cycle of a flock. Don't interfere unless a bird is being harmed to the point that blood is drawn. It is hard to watch, but you must observe in case it gets out of control.

Here are some helpful tips for introducing new birds:

- Introduce chickens that are the same size as those in your existing flock.
- Make sure there is enough room in your coop and at the feeders for the increased number of birds. Overcrowding stresses birds and makes them less tolerant of newcomers.
- Make hiding places for the new birds. Set up a few boxes or make a shelter of tree branches in the chicken yard.
- Plan to cull or sell any bird that is so aggressive it doesn't allow any newcomers or is aggressive toward you or any member of your family.

There are a few different methods of introducing new birds to a flock after the quarantine period. Try these methods and find the ones that work best for your setup.

Keeping too many roosters in a backyard flock leads to fighting among the roosters. Here the dominant white cock looks healthy and in good condition, while the lower-ranking red cock looks beat-up and has lost all of his tail feathers. This is a result of the pecking, a social order that happens in all chicken flocks. *Corallina Breuer*

1. Take your dominant bird out of the flock and let the other birds work out the social order first, then reintroduce your dominant bird. This helps cut down on the total aggression toward the new birds all at once.

2. Cage the newcomers within your coop. All birds can meet each other but not touch. The cage helps keep the aggression in check. Plan on this setup for a day or two, and then combine all of the birds.

3. If you allow your flock to free-range, let the newcomers loose for a few hours and then release the established flock members. The newcomers will get to know the area and find hiding spots, if needed.

4. Move both groups to a new coop at the same time. This makes everyone feel like a newcomer, since it is unfamiliar to all. Neither group will have established ownership, and everyone will be on equal, unfamiliar footing.

5. Try putting new chickens on the roosts in the coop after dark when the established flock is settled down. At first light they will all wake up together and go about their regular business. The pecking order will still have to be worked out, but it should be less aggressive toward the newcomers.

Daily Chores

Set a time during the day to do your chicken chores. A consistent schedule will help you remember them. Plan ahead to have another family member or a friend take care of your flock if you know you will be gone or extra busy on a certain day. Your daily chores should include the following:

- Filling waterers daily
- Filling feeders daily
- Collecting eggs twice daily
- Opening the coop into a fenced yard or free-ranging access door
- Observing all birds for signs of ill health or stress
- Closing the coop at dusk

Weekly Chores

Pick a certain day of the week when you have the most time available to complete the weekly chores, and then stick to that schedule. Weekly chores related to caring for your flock include the following:

- Refilling grit and oyster shell feeders
- Disinfecting waterers or an automatic watering system
- Making a list of any supplies needed for the coming week

A hutch like this can be used for many types of small animals. It has enough square footage for a pair of large fowl birds or four bantam birds. It requires extra weather protection by being placed inside a shed or garage. It is elevated for easy access and so you can see the birds. *Tara Kindschi*

- Adding more bedding to nesting boxes
- Checking floor bedding and adding more or removing soiled bedding as needed

Culling the Flock

Culling is the act of removing nonproductive or diseased birds from your flock. You can cull birds at any age. You can sell, butcher, or euthanize (humanely kill) your extra birds. Check your state and local regulations before selling live birds, meat products, or eggs.

What birds should you consider culling?
Extra Cockerels

If you purchased straight-run chicks and plan on keeping only one or no roosters, your best meat quality will come while the cockerels are under six months of age. Too many roosters will continually fight for dominance and the females, and it doesn't take long until none of the birds are happy or healthy. Use the criteria for selecting a bird to show listed in Chapter 8 to determine which is your best male in each breed and keep him only. If space is limited and you don't plan to keep any birds in separate pens, one male per one to twenty females is sufficient for fertility.

Older Birds

A chicken can easily live twelve years or more. A hen's most productive laying period is from nine months to two years of age. After that, depending on her breed, genetics, and environmental conditions, she will continue to lay eggs, but fewer will be produced. She'll still eat the same amount of feed and take up the same space in your coop. A cock may remain fertile his entire life or may become sterile due to extreme weather conditions or loss of his physical ability to catch and properly mount the females. His territorial instincts and hormones may make him more aggressive toward other birds and humans as he ages.

This hen shows the result of too many roosters in the flock. She has been mated so many times that the feathers on the back of her head and back have been pulled out or broken off. This situation can be remedied by culling excess males or keeping males and females in separate pens. This hen's feathers will probably not grow back in until her next molt. *Corallina Breuer*

Lackluster Birds

If you have a bird or a few birds that continually seem droopy and have poor growth rates, consider culling them. They may have bad hearts, have organ damage, be genetically inferior, or have any number of other things wrong that only a costly biopsy after death will show. After carefully reviewing the chicken diseases section in Chapter 6, if you determine they are not suffering from something treatable, remove them from your flock.

Aggressive Birds

Consider getting rid of any bird that continually attacks you or another family member. There is no joy in being chased or cornered by an aggressive bird. These birds are usually males guarding their flock. They have strong territorial instincts that are impossible to break once they start exerting them. This may also be the case if you have more than one male and they don't get along with each other. The constant fighting and wounds that may result do not allow a good quality of life for either bird. Just keep one male in your small flock.

Egg-Eaters

This bad habit can develop in hens that accidentally break an egg while on a nest and then eat it. They like the taste and soon learn to break more eggs to eat. This is a habit that is impossible to cure. Hens with this habit should be culled as soon as you discover the problem.

Birds with Defects

If you have a laying hen flock, birds with defects may be fine to keep. On the other hand, if you plan to show or breed chickens, birds with defects won't be of use to you. Review the list of defects and disqualifications in Chapter 7 and handle each of your birds

This bantam cockerel red Turken exhibits two major problems. His single comb is lopped (a disqualification at shows), and many of his comb points will be lost due to his recent case of frostbite from harsh winter temperatures. *Kendall Babcock*

to determine if they have any problems that would bar them from competition.

What can you do with culled birds?
Butcher

Extensive studies have shown that raising extra cockerels of egg-laying breeds for resale as meat products is not economically feasible. While their taste can't be beaten, the amount of feed consumed, the length of time to maturity, and the processing costs are all too high for any good return on your investment. Store-bought chicken pieces consist of broiler-meat crosses. Broilers produce a much larger breast area and meat-to-carcass ratio in a shorter timeframe. Free-range and locally grown meat crosses have the same body type as the chicken you see for sale in stores. There are meat processing plants that butcher any type of chicken, but they charge per the bird and not the pound. This means that your six-month-old cockerel weighing four to six pounds will cost the same to process as a ten-pound roaster and give you a much higher per-pound processing cost.

Home butchering is a cheaper option but can be very messy and time consuming. All of your knives and work areas should be clean and sanitized between batches. The process involves removing feed from your birds for one day before slaughter. The bird is killed by removing the head and allowing the body to bleed out by hanging it by the feet for several minutes. The feathers need to be removed from the skin by dipping the carcass in scalding hot water for a few minutes then using a plucking machine or pulling the feathers out by hand. This process of dipping the carcass in the hot water and pulling feathers may need to be repeated until all the feathers have been removed. Then the internal organs need to be removed from the crop (gizzard) on down by cutting and pulling them out through the vent area. This process is very tricky, since you don't want to cut through any internal organs with juices that can spoil the meat, but you still want to clean out the body cavity completely. The heart, crop, and liver are usually saved for consumption. The final step is to remove the legs and feet and cut the bird into sections or leave the carcass in one piece, depending on your cooking preference. Then the bird can be cooked and eaten or bagged and frozen for future use. It is important to cool the bird quickly after slaughter to control bacteria growth.

Meat from an older bird tends to get tough and stringy, but birds over one year of age can also be eaten if prepared properly. A longer cooking time and more moisture will tenderize the meat for use in soups and casseroles. This is where the term "stew hen" came from. A flock keeper would stew older hens when their prime productive laying time was finished. Skinning a bird instead of plucking the feathers speeds up and simplifies the home butchering process. A different cooking method will need to be used to keep the meat of a skinned hen from drying out, which is the main purpose of leaving skin on when baking and frying younger birds.

Sell to Other Poultry Keepers

If you have excess pullets, finding a buyer is usually easy by using word of mouth. You can also place a sign at your local feed store or post a notice on poultry Internet sites. It's difficult to find a buyer for extra males and old hens, and you shouldn't try to pass off problem birds to others.

Ethnic Market Sales

There is an increasing interest in several ethnic populations for live birds for food and religious customs. Their wants and needs with regard to breeds and sizes are quite specific and different from traditional American tastes. Learn where ethnic populations reside and become familiar with their basic customs and holiday times. This market can be the easiest way to get rid of your unwanted birds. You won't make a profit selling birds to ethnic markets, but you will keep your feed costs lower and your coop from becoming overcrowded.

Euthanize Birds

Euthanizing should be your only choice for diseased birds that don't completely recover from a disease outbreak or become disease carriers. Do not pass these birds off to an unwary buyer. If the birds have been treated with any medications, they are not suitable for human or animal consumption for up to 21 days. Whether you euthanize the bird by removing its head, by placing its head under water, or by having a veterinarian give a lethal injection, proper disposal of the body is imperative to prevent further disease outbreaks. Cremation is recommended.

Is It a Hen or a Rooster?

Listening for crowing to determine a chicken's sex can be a long wait and a very early morning experiment. Looking at the comb doesn't work well either, since some breeds, such as Leghorns, have huge, red single combs on both sexes, while Wyandotte breeds have compact, close-to-the-head rose combs on both sexes. There is an easier method to identify a bird's sex that works for over 95 percent of the breeds and crossbreeds. Take a close look at a feather from the hackle or saddle area (refer to the chicken conformation diagram if needed) and look at the end of the feather. If it is pointed and shaped like an arrow, you have a male. Females have a curved, spoon-shaped end. A few breeds are classified as hen-feathered, however, which means both sexes have the curved feather of a female. Sebright Bantams are an example of this exception to the feather-shape rule. Silkies have a missing barb in their feathers that keeps you from seeing the feather end clearly. Regardless of these exceptions, taking a close look at the feather is still the best method to determine the sex of your bird.

Record Keeping

Proper management of a chicken flock, whether large or small, is a detailed project. Written records are helpful in making budgets, for changing the scope or scale of the project, and for remembering mistakes and accomplishments from previous years.

Starting a simple record-keeping system in a notebook or three-ring binder will be useful for future flock care and to assist young people in filling out their 4-H project books. Items for your record-keeping system should include the following:

Photos
- Your chicks as they grow
- A particular breed you saw and would like to purchase
- Trophies or ribbons you won

Brochures
- New hatchery catalogs
- Show entry catalogs

To-Do List
- Improvements you wish to make to your coop
- Items for showing that you need
- Schedules for worming, vaccinations, and blood testing, plus show dates

Keep an inventory of the birds you have, including age, sex, and band number. Also include a list of breeds you have liked and breeds that didn't work well for you.

Cochins come in many color varieties. This small flock of bantams includes blacks, blues, and a black frizzle. Their feathered legs and feet require extra care to stay in show condition. Free-ranging or dirt yards are not recommended for these varieties, since their toe feathers are easily soiled or broken. *Corallina Breuer*

HOUSING REQUIREMENTS

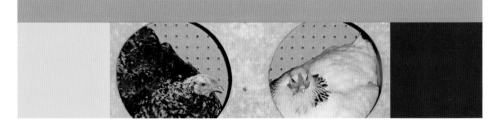

C hickens are adaptable creatures. Any housing you provide that meets their basic needs will work. Chickens are social animals and are happiest with others like themselves. A pair or trio of birds can have their space needs met in a variety of simple cages, while a traditional coop is a good plan for up to twenty-five hens.

Old structures can take on a new life. The structure is sound, and some modifications can easily make this into a workable chicken coop. This type of structure is often advertised as free for the removal. Placing the coop on a cement pad will offer protection from rodents and predators. *DeAnn Richards*

The same chicken coop looks quite different after modifications and new siding. The larger and more secure window system helps with lighting and protection from predators. Special care should be taken to disinfect older coops before housing new flocks, since many diseases and some parasites can live in a coop's cracks for years. *DeAnn Richards*

Chicken Coops

The most common housing for chickens is a coop. It can be a new construction or a converted tool shed, old garage, or playhouse. The main purpose of a chicken coop is to provide housing and a space to allow your birds to move about freely on the ground. It's also a place to collect eggs and feed and water your birds. An attached outside yard is a bonus. Plan to allow a minimum space of 2 to 2.5 square feet per bird for large fowl and 1 to 1.5 square feet per bird for bantams.

You can place a chicken coop in your backyard if your local zoning laws will allow it. Be sure to check with your neighbors before you buy any chickens. Most city zoning laws don't permit roosters. Keeping birds on your property and offering some extra eggs to your neighbors can create a great boost to the community. *Kelly Damaschke*

Predator Protection

Daytime predators can be as much of a problem for your flock as nighttime predators. You may think of hawks, foxes, or raccoons as common threats, but dogs are the number one predator of backyard flocks. Whether it is your own dog, a neighbor's, or a stray, the results can be devastating in the number of casualties in a single dog attack. A chicken coop with a very small access door to the yard can give chickens a place to hide.

A closed chicken coop will help keep your flock safe from nighttime predators, such as owls and raccoons, that would otherwise find your flock to be a tasty midnight snack. Closing your coop every night by dusk is the

This newly built chicken coop with attached yard is constructed from recycled barn boards and other materials. The south-facing windows and access door are all open on nice summer days but will be shut by dusk to keep the chickens safe from night predators. *Corallina Breuer*

Dogs are the number one predator of chickens. Breeds like this collie use their herding instincts to chase and herd the birds until they get tired and are caught. Hunting dogs see the chickens as targets that must be captured. Take precautions to protect your flock from dogs, either your own or others. *Tara Kindschi*

best way to keep your birds safe. If you know you will be out late one night or are going on vacation, leave your birds in the coop all day for their protection.

Any windows or vents that open to the outside of the chicken coop should be covered in heavy wire with the staples on the inside of the house to prevent predators, such as raccoons, from pulling the staples out and entering the coop. Dogs and raccoons also may try to get at your flock by digging under an outside fenced area next to the coop. Be sure to bury the bottom of any fence at least six inches into the ground and close all doors to the coop at night, even if the outside fenced area is covered.

This newly constructed chicken coop is designed for a multitude of uses. It can be used to grow out small numbers of birds or hold a breeding pair or trio, or keep males separate. It features a covered outside yard for predator protection and shade from the sun. The inner area is perfect for egg laying and night roosting. *ACA Hady Poultry*

Coop Housing Specifications

A coop must provide basic protection for your flock's health and well-being. It must be designed or remodeled based on the following basic housing requirements.

Draft Free

Chickens can tolerate cold and wet conditions outside their coop if the inside is dry and draft free. There needs to be airflow in a coop, but direct drafts, such as those coming from an open screened window, should be avoided on a breezy winter day.

Ventilation

Bird waste creates a lot of odor and excess moisture in your coop. Deep, clean bedding helps control this, but the air must be able to leave the coop without causing a direct draft. This is best accomplished by a vent system

Make modifications if you see your birds not using or struggling with a part of their coop. These hens were slipping on the board ramp, so crossbars were added so they could better enter and exit the hen house. Watch your birds and their daily habits so you will know if something is not right in their environment. *Shelly Sonsalla*

in the roof or high on the back side of the coop. If your bedding is continually damp or frozen solid in the winter, your coop needs more ventilation.

Floor

A wooden or concrete floor is preferable to a dirt floor for several reasons. Dirt and gravel can retain bacteria that can cause disease, and it is impossible to disinfect your coop completely if there is any type of outbreak. With dirt floors, predators can burrow under your coop walls and have access to your flock any time of the day. Rodents, such as mice and rats, will burrow deep tunnels under the bedding and live happily, produce many offspring, and contaminate the feed, and they may even attack your birds.

Lighting

Chickens enjoy natural sunlight. The best way to maximize this light is to have several large windows on the south side of your coop. To keep your hens laying year-round, plan to supplement daylight with electric lighting on a timer system. Give your hens twelve to sixteen hours of light a day for maximum laying ability.

Electricity

While not mandatory, electricity is needed when using a light and timer system to keep

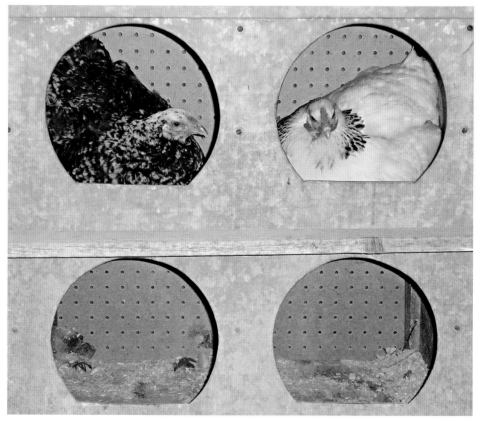

Nesting boxes should be well placed in the coop. There should be one hole for every four to six hens. This traditional nesting unit comes in four-, eight-, and twelve-hole versions. Any unit you buy or make should have a landing board to assist the hens with getting in and out of the nest holes. *Kelly Damaschke*

your hens laying during the winter. Outlets for plugging in a heated water base or electric fencing are also helpful.

Separate Species

Plan to use your coop for chickens only. Waterfowl are very messy and will continually dirty the waterers. They can be very aggressive and dominate even the biggest chicken. Plus they require different feed. Pigeons, turkeys, and guineas are also not a good mix for your chicken flock. Turkeys are much larger than chickens and will dominate at the feeder. Turkeys are also highly susceptible to many diseases chickens carry but that don't make the chickens sick. Male guineas are very aggressive with chickens and will kill them in territorial fights. Pigeons have very different nutrient requirements and are carriers of lice and mites.

Chicken Yard

A yard or fenced-in area attached to your chicken coop is an added bonus for your birds. Make sure the area is predator-safe and that heavy wire is used and buried at least six inches into the ground. A top wire or bird netting over the entire yard will help keep flying and climbing predators, such as hawks and raccoons, out of the yard. It may also prove useful in keeping any of your gamey, flighty breeds from flying out. Adding a strand of electric fence around the top of the fence and along the bottom edge on the outside may also help deter predators, such as foxes and dogs.

Make sure your chicken yard is placed in a well-drained area with protection from the hot afternoon sun. This protection can be either natural shade from a tree, shade from

A red Turken cock shows off for the hens. Notice the converted dog-kennel-type system used to give hens access to the outside. The wire is not buried in the ground, so digging predators, such as raccoons or dogs, could gain access through this yard. *Corallina Breuer*

These young bantams are taking a dust bath. All chickens that are free-range or have access to a dirt yard will want to dust-bathe. This is one way chickens clean their feathers and get rid of external parasites. *Shelly Sonsalla*

the coop itself, or shade netting that is sold commercially.

The yard is the ideal place to have an area where your chickens can dust-bathe. Chickens will naturally try to do this wherever they are kept. You can encourage this instinct and also keep the holes away from fence edges if you set up the bathing area yourself. Use a shovel to dig a four- to six-inch-deep hole that is twelve to eighteen inches across. Replace that dirt with clean sand and add enough extra sand to form a small mound. When the chickens find this spot, they will literally dig in and use their wings and feet to work the loose sand between their feathers. This process helps the birds remove lice, mites, and dirt from their feathers. When they are done bathing, they stand up, ruffle all their feathers, and shake the dirt out. Occasionally add more sand to make sure they have enough to bathe.

The chicken yard is also a great spot for putting extra table scraps (except meat),

garden waste, and lawn clippings. The birds can pick out everything edible for them, and you can easily remove woody stems and uneaten waste without messing up the coop.

Are you having trouble with birds flying out of their coop or enclosure? You can clip their wing feathers to prevent this. While holding the wing with its feathers spread out, start trimming the primary wing feathers with a very sharp pair of scissors. Trim a half of an inch at a time until the center feather shaft starts to look pink. Stop when you get to this point. Trimming the feathers will not hurt the bird unless you get into the pink/blood area of the feathers. This method is not permanent. The procedure must be repeated when new feathers grow in after a molt.

The inside view of a hen house shows an access door open for egg collection and nest box cleaning. The door along the roofline also opens for roost cleaning and catching birds. A heat lamp can be added to this setup for cold days when the birds don't want to venture outside. *Shelly Sonsalla*

This inside view of a hen house roosting system at dusk shows enough headroom for even this rather large light Brahma hen. If used for bantams, the headroom could be kept the same, or the roof line could be slightly lowered. *Shelly Sonsalla*

Alternative Housing

Hen House

A hen house is a bit different than a chicken coop, but you may find the two terms used interchangeably. A hen house is only large enough for the birds to enter and live in. It does not have enough headroom for a person or child to enter. Access doors from the outside allow for egg collection and cleaning. Depending on climate and weather conditions, this house may be set up for the feeders and waterers to be placed outside. The small size of a hen house is a housing option for flocks kept in urban areas or for people who move a lot, since the hen house can easily be moved. They are often built to hold four to six chickens. Larger units or groupings of these houses will work for a bigger flock.

Chicken Tractor

The chicken tractor system is great for raising meat birds and also is appropriate for a small laying flock. The "tractor" is a movable, open-bottomed pen that confines the birds to a limited space in tall grass or weeds where they can free-range for the majority of their food. The pen is moved daily. A pen should be tall enough to allow laying hens to roost a few inches off the ground. Build nesting boxes on a side to collect eggs. This system works well in warm climates and seasonally in northern regions.

Caging System

Large, commercial egg farms are set up with caging systems that hold one hen per cage. The cages are stacked two to four deep in long rows in a single building that can hold more

This is a close-up view of a commercial laying hen setup for the feed, watering, and egg collection systems. The breed shown appears to be a commercial strain of single-comb white Leghorns. The egg in front of every hen indicates this breed's superb egg production. *Corallina Breuer*

than five thousand hens. There are catch pans for the droppings and automatic feeding, watering, and egg-collection systems.

Backyard chickens can be raised entirely in wire cages, either singly or in small groups. Reasons to raise or keep chickens in a cage include the following:

- Keep the males separate to prevent fighting.
- Allow a sick or injured bird to recover without being picked on by flockmates.
- Give broody hens needed private space.
- Keep feather-leg breeds from damaging or dirtying their feet feathers on the ground.
- Set up small breeding pens consisting of one male and one to four females.

Housing Combinations

Most avid poultry enthusiasts have a variety of housing available to meet the flock's needs. Have areas that are adaptable to different situations. For example, a large cage with a wire floor can be built with enough headroom for a large fowl trio to use as a breeding pen in late winter. That same cage could also be used to provide enough square footage and predator protection to raise six to twelve full-feathered chicks to adulthood in the spring.

A variety of cages can be used to house chickens. Large dog and rabbit cages are being used here for breeding pairs. Filling the many waterers and feeders for this housing system can be a time-consuming daily chore. Bedding needs to be cleaned out on a weekly basis or more frequently whenever it becomes damp or soiled. *DeAnn Richards*

Large rabbit cages are suitable to use for chickens. Make sure there is enough height for whatever breed you choose to be able to use a roost without touching their combs to the top of the cage. The roost doesn't have to be high. It can be as little as two inches off the floor.

House Pet

There has been an increasing popularity in recent years of people raising a single chicken as a house pet. Chicken diapers are sold by some mail-order supply houses, since chickens are not house-trainable like a dog or cat. If you raise an adult chicken in the house, use caution because their nails are not meant for hard surfaces, and walking can be a problem. Also remember that chickens are social creatures and will thrive best when raised with other chickens.

Free-ranging chickens roost and dig in many places, sometimes where they aren't supposed to be. A fenced chicken yard with covered top is a nice alternative. This red pyle Old English Game cock considered a vehicle in his yard to be a good resting spot. *Kelly Damaschke*

CHICKEN MANAGEMENT

This large fowl, black Cochin cockerel is in prime feather condition and health. Good sanitation and quarantine practices are required to maintain your flock's health, especially when birds are brought into the flock that may have been exposed to diseases or parasites from other birds. *Kelly Damaschke*

Good management of your chicken flock requires attention to many details. Even when you carefully attend to all the daily details of raising your flock, things can go wrong. Being responsible for a flock of chickens also means knowing how to respond when the unexpected happens. A favorite bird could get sick, or a raccoon could attack and kill or injure some of your birds. You can take several steps to be prepared for emergency situations.

Be Prepared

Being prepared for possible injuries and sickness of your birds is part of a flock keeper's role. Put together a box that contains the supplies you'll need to help in such a situation. The box itself can be a purchased toolbox, a handmade wooden box, or a sturdy cardboard container that you clearly mark as your poultry box. Plan to include the following items:

- Sterile gauze, tape, and scissors for covering flesh wounds
- Syringes in 1cc and 3cc sizes
- Needles to fit the syringes
- Rubbing alcohol for cleaning syringes and needles between birds
- Cotton balls for cleaning off blood and cleaning needles
- Amprol or Corid powder (both contain Amprolium), which is a treatment for coccidiosis
- Triple antibiotic ointment for skin irritations and wounds from predator attacks
- Water-soluble antibiotic
- Water-soluble probiotic/electrolyte
- Disinfectant. Oxine has more uses than simple bleach. It can be used as a cleanser and a fog in cases of fungal infections.

You should also have vaccines for Marek's disease, fowl pox, and perhaps other diseases that are prevalent in your area. Check with your veterinarian as to what is most applicable for your flock. The vaccines should be refrigerated.

Disease Prevention

Taking care of your flock is a daily chore that can have many rewards, along with a few drawbacks. The first sign of illness can be as simple as birds eating or drinking less and general sluggishness. Illnesses can also happen quickly with an infection that takes healthy birds to a state of breathing difficulty or death in a day or less.

Prevention Precautions

- Use caution with medications
- Know what illness you are treating
- Follow dosage and treatment times
- Follow withdrawal times for meat and eggs
- Only use medications labeled for use in poultry

Disease prevention should be a primary focus at all times. Prevention techniques will pay for themselves many times over in the long run by helping you avoid a disease outbreak and loss in your flock or the spread of disease to another flock.

This young bird is not healthy. All symptoms must be noted for a veterinarian or poultry expert to determine the specific disease the bird or flock has and how to treat it. In some cases, tests may be required to determine the cause of illness or death of a bird. *Kendall Babcock*

in unvaccinated poultry flocks, and the virus can sometimes infect and cause death even in vaccinated birds.

Exotic Newcastle disease affects the respiratory, nervous, and digestive systems and will incubate for two to fifteen days. Symptoms may include the following: sneezing; difficulty breathing; nasal discharge; coughing; greenish, watery diarrhea; signs of depression; tremors in the muscles; drooping wings; head and neck twisting; circling; complete paralysis; drop in number of eggs laid; laying of thin-shelled eggs; swelling of the tissues around the eyes and in the neck; sudden death; and increased number of deaths in a flock.

The disease spreads to healthy birds when they come in contact with the bodily fluids of infected birds. Material infected with the virus can be carried on shoes and clothing from an infected flock to a healthy flock. Poultry farm owners, farm employees, work crews, delivery personnel, buyers, drivers, and service people often speed the spread of disease throughout commercial poultry operations.

The virus can survive on feathers, manure, and other objects for several weeks in a warm and humid environment. It can survive indefinitely in frozen material. However, the virus is destroyed by dry conditions and ultraviolet sunlight.

Fowl Typhoid (Salmonella Gallinarum)

Fowl typhoid is an infectious, contagious bacterial disease that is usually mild but can be severe. It can infect most domestic and wild fowl, including chickens. It should not be confused with typhoid fever in humans, however, which is caused by a very different organism.

Fowl typhoid is transmitted by an infected hen to her egg, from an egg to a chick, or from chick to chick. Once infected, the bird is always an infected breeder, and the cycle

continues. The disease can also be transmitted by clothing, shoes, or equipment, or in any living area that wasn't disinfected after a previous outbreak.

Birds of any age can be infected, but the disease primarily occurs in juveniles (usually those older than twelve weeks of age). Average death loss varies from very few birds to about 40 percent. Symptoms include sudden death, sluggishness, green or yellow diarrhea (accompanied by pasty butt), loss of appetite, increased thirst, and a pale, weak appearance of the comb and wattles.

Prevention and control of fowl typhoid is more successful when basic disease prevention practices are followed closely, including testing flocks for the disease before hatching chicks from them, keeping the farm carefully clean and free from contamination, providing fresh feed and water, and disposing of all dead birds properly. Thoroughly disinfect the premises after an outbreak, and when possible, rotate your range area to prevent the infection from carrying over to the following flock.

Drugs cannot prevent typhoid effectively and are not recommended, but infected birds may be treated using the same drugs used to treat pullorum-infected birds.

Infectious Bronchitis

Infectious bronchitis is an extremely contagious respiratory disease caused by a virus that only affects chickens. It is considered the most contagious poultry disease, and when it occurs, all birds on the farm are vulnerable, regardless of sanitary or quarantine precautions. The disease can be spread by clothing, poultry crates, and equipment, but it can also spread through the air and travel considerable distances during an active outbreak. Infectious bronchitis is not egg transmitted, however, and the virus will survive for probably no more than a week in an empty coop. The virus is also easily destroyed by heat and ordinary disinfectants.

The infection is confined to the respiratory system, and symptoms usually include difficultly breathing, gasping, sneezing, and wheezing. Though some birds may have a slight watery nasal discharge, the disease never causes problems with the nervous system. The illness lasts for ten to fourteen days in a flock, so you will know that symptoms that last longer than two weeks are from some other cause.

Death rates from bronchitis in young chickens under three weeks old can be as high as 30 or 40 percent, but the disease does not cause a significant number of deaths in birds over five weeks of age. When bronchitis infects a laying flock, egg production usually drops to near zero within a few days. It may take four weeks or more before the flock returns to production, and some flocks never regain their previous laying rate. Small, soft-shelled, irregular-shaped eggs are sometimes produced during an outbreak.

Infectious bronchitis is difficult to diagnose, since it is similar to many of the other respiratory diseases. Because of this, lab tests are usually required to get a definite diagnosis. This disease is highly contagious and cannot always be controlled by sanitation. There is also no treatment for this disease, so vaccinate the chickens you plan to keep as layers. Numerous vaccines are available commercially.

Infectious Coryza

Infectious coryza is a respiratory disease specific to chickens that generally occurs in semi-mature or adult birds. Infection may be a slow-spreading, chronic disease that affects a small number of birds at a time, or it can appear as a rapidly spreading disease with more birds affected. Infectious coryza is not a widespread disease, however, so the chances of it affecting your flock are relatively low.

Outbreaks of this bacterial disease usually result from the introduction of infected or carrier birds into a flock. The bacteria can be transmitted by direct contact, by airborne infection, or by contaminated drinking water, and birds usually develop symptoms within three days after being exposed to the disease. Chickens that recover may appear normal, but they will remain carriers of the organism for a long period of time, so once a flock is infected, all birds must be considered carriers.

The most common symptoms of infectious coryza include a swollen face around the eyes and wattles, nasal discharge, and swollen sinuses. Watery discharge from the eyes often causes the lids to stick together. Diagnosis can only be confirmed by isolating and identifying the bacteria that trigger the disease, and infection can usually be prevented by eliminating contact between healthy and infected or carrier birds. Introduce started or adult birds only from sources known to be free of the infection, and if infection occurs, remove all the birds and then clean and disinfect the entire area thoroughly.

A number of drugs are effective for treating the symptoms of the disease, although the disease is never completely gone. You can put sulfadimethoxine or sulfathiazole in the feed or water or erythromycin in the drinking water to reduce the symptoms of this disease.

Marek's Disease

Marek's disease usually only occurs in young chickens, but older birds can also be affected. The disease is caused by a virus belonging to the herpes group, a virus that is concentrated in the feathers, shed in the dander, and spread by inhaling the dander. The virus has a long survival time and can be found in coops that have been left empty for many months.

One type of the disease is characterized by lesions on the gonads, liver, kidneys, and spleen. The disease often goes unnoticed, with what appear to be healthy birds dying very quickly of huge internal tumors. Marek's may appear in broiler-age birds, but the highest death rates usually occur in new pullets that haven't yet begun egg production.

The other type of Marek's is known for its progressive paralyzing effect on the wings, legs, and neck. Weight loss, anemia, difficulty breathing, and diarrhea are common symptoms. Lesions aren't common with this type of the disease, however.

Diagnosis is based upon the flock's history and signs of the disease. An accurate diagnosis may depend on lab results. There is no treatment for Marek's disease, but a very effective vaccine, with a 90 percent success rate, is available. The vaccine is administered to day-old chicks as an injection under the skin, and it requires that you strictly follow the manufacturer's recommendations, including the use of a sterile environment during injection. If you buy your chicks from a hatchery, they receive the vaccine before they are shipped to you. If your chicks are raised at home, carefully read the manufacturer's recommendations or talk to your local veterinarian.

Moniliasis (Thrush)

This disease, caused by a yeast-like fungus, primarily affects the upper digestive tract of all birds and is characterized by whitish, thickened areas of the crop; a thin gizzard lining; and inflammation of the vent area. Chickens, domestic animals, and humans of all ages are susceptible to this organism that is widely spread throughout the world.

Moniliasis is transmitted by ingesting the fungus through infected feed, water, or the environment (dirt, feces, etc.). Unsanitary and dirty water troughs are excellent homes for the organism, and the fungus also grows especially well on corn. The disease does not spread directly from bird to bird.

Thrush does not produce very specific symptoms. Young birds become listless and pale, show ruffled feathers, and appear generally unhealthy. Affected egg-layers become overweight and anemic. Some birds have a whitish incrustation of the feathers and skin around the vent area that resembles a diarrhea-induced condition. Birds may consume 10 to 20 percent more feed.

Lesions are usually only on the crop and gizzard. The crop has whitish, thickened areas that are often described as having a "Turkish towel" appearance, which means they look like a bath towel material that consists of small loops. The gizzard lining is often thin, and the intestines are inflamed. Diagnosis is based on the flock's history and symptoms. The condition is confirmed by isolation and lab tests.

You can treat your flock with an antimycotic drug, which will control the infection. Many antibiotics will make the symptoms worse and should not be used until after the infection is under control.

Once moniliasis is introduced into the flock, it is spread by poor management conditions. Preventative measures include using additives to reduce mold in the feed, handling and storing feed properly, cleaning and sanitizing the watering system daily, and refreshing the bedding periodically or replacing wet bedding to prevent caking. As an inexpensive, yet effective, water treatment, you can add household chlorine bleach to the drinking water at the rate of five parts per million (ppm). That breaks down to one tablespoon per gallon.

Mycoplasmosis (CRD, Air Sac Syndrome, Sinusitis)

Mycoplasma organisms are a major cause of poultry respiratory disease. Three are very important and cause the most damage to chickens. One is associated with chronic respiratory disease (CRD), another causes air sac syndrome, and the other is associated with infectious sinusitis.

CRD was first recognized as a chronic but mild respiratory disease that affected adult chickens. It reduced egg production but caused few deaths. Then a condition known as air sac syndrome became a problem in young birds, causing high death rates in some flocks. The birds in these flocks don't grow or eat well, and many fowl must be rejected for human consumption.

CRD produces slight respiratory symptoms, such as coughing, sneezing, and runny nose. However, the entire respiratory system is affected with air sac syndrome. Affected birds become droopy, don't eat, and quickly lose weight.

Diagnosis of a mycoplasmosis condition must be based on flock history and symptoms. Blood tests are also useful in determining whether a flock is infected. Many antibiotics have been used with varying success, but the decision to treat your flock or not must be made based on how much it will cost. If you decide to treat your birds, give high levels of one of the broad-spectrum antibiotics by adding it to feed or drinking water, or by giving injections. The form of infectious sinusitis that affects the upper respiratory system can be successfully treated by injecting antibiotics into the swollen sinuses.

Mycotoxicosis

Mycotoxicosis is caused by eating toxic substances produced by molds growing on feed, feed ingredients, and bedding. There are several toxins that may cause problems in poultry, but aflatoxins are the most serious. Under certain conditions, the aflatoxins cause reduced growth, egg production, and hatchability of those eggs; physiological stress; a reduced ability to develop immunity; and even death. This illness is hard to diagnose because the lesions are usually not present, and detecting the toxin doesn't mean that it is the cause of the problems.

Molds are everywhere in nature. Grains and feed frequently become infected with toxin-producing molds before they are harvested. The key to reducing mold growth is to control moisture and temperature while storing feed. The mold, though present, cannot produce toxic products unless allowed to grow freely. Aflatoxins in feeds can be detected by chemical tests, but once the toxin is produced, there is no way to remove it from the feed. If your feed supply is infected, you will have to destroy it.

Necrotic Enteritis

Necrotic enteritis destroys the intestinal lining of the digestive tract. The disease is also called rot gut, crud, and cauliflower gut, terms that accurately describe the appearance and effects of the condition. The primary cause of the disease is a spore-forming bacterium, but coccidiosis may be a contributing factor. Toxins produced by bacteria apparently cause most of the damage to the intestines.

Little is known about how the disease spreads, but it may be transmitted through contact with the droppings from infected birds. Necrotic enteritis appears suddenly and causes apparently healthy birds to become very depressed and die within hours. The death rate is usually between 2 and 10 percent but may be as high as 30 percent in severe outbreaks, and losses from slow growth and feed conversion may be more expensive than having part of your flock die.

The disease usually involves the lower half of the small intestine, but in some cases the entire bowel is affected. The intestine is expanded and contains a dark fluid and a cauliflower-like membrane. The intestinal lining will look coarse, and bits may break off and pass out in the bird's feces.

CHICKEN MANAGEMENT

mainly transmitted through eggs, but it can be transmitted from an infected hen to an egg, from an egg to a chick, or from chick to chick in an incubator, chick box, brooder, or house. The survivors (carrier birds that look healthy) become infected breeders, and the cycle is repeated. It can also be transmitted on clothes, shoes, or equipment, and areas that are not disinfected from a previous outbreak can also transmit the disease.

The infection may enter the bird through the respiratory or digestive systems, and most outbreaks begin with birds that were infected while in the hatchery. Pullorum disease is very fatal to young chicks, but mature birds have a higher resistance. Infected chicks may die soon after hatching without showing any signs of infection. Most acute outbreaks occur in birds that are under three weeks of age, with death rates in such outbreaks approaching 90 percent if left untreated. Survivors are usually small and thin. Young birds often show symptoms like droopiness, ruffled feathers, appearing chilled and huddled near a heat source, difficulty breathing, and white diarrhea or pasty butt.

Diagnosis in young birds is determined by lab testing. Blood testing may indicate an infection in older birds, but a positive diagnosis here also depends upon lab tests. Complete elimination of all birds in an infected flock is the only way to prevent pullorum disease. All birds supplied by a hatchery should be tested, and only pullorum-free flocks should be used to hatch eggs. Purchase chicks from hatcheries that are officially recognized as "pullorum clean."

Some of the drugs used to treat pullorum disease are furazolidone, gentamicin sulfate, and sulfa drugs (sulfadimethoxine, sulfamethazine, and sulfamerazine). Treatment will only save your birds, however. It does not prevent them from becoming carriers. Do not keep birds that have

recovered from pullorum if you plan to use them for egg production.

Chicken Parasites

Parasites can be broken down into two main categories: those that feed externally and those that feed internally. There are many insecticides available to help control external poultry parasites. The most effective broad-spectrum insecticide is permethrin, which is used in a spray form. It can be used to treat the coop, equipment, and birds. Carefully follow all manufacturer recommendations when using all insecticides. The treatment should be repeated on a one- to two-month schedule or whenever mites are detected.

This white-crested black Polish hen's crest shows an extreme infestation of multiple types of mites. Notice the scabs formed from the irritation and blood-sucking habits of the mites. Treatment of an advanced case like this should begin immediately, with follow-up treatment every two to three weeks to catch any mites that may hatch from eggs already laid. Bathing the chicken a few days after treatment will help remove a large portion of the dead and dying mites and offer some comfort to the bird. *Kendall Babcock*

This is an example of an extreme, untreated case of scaly leg mites. The mites' droppings build up on the shanks and toes and cause the scales to expand. The deposits harden like concrete. Scaly leg mites are usually passed as a result of direct contact with an infected bird. They should be treated as soon as they are noticed. *Kendall Babcock*

External Parasites

Poultry Mites

Chickens are susceptible to mites. Some mites suck blood, while others burrow in the skin or live in the feathers. These mites cause slow growth rates, reduced egg production, sluggishness, damaged feathers, and even death in severe cases. Mites are very small, and you must look closely to see them on your birds. Following are a few specific types of mites.

Northern Fowl Mite

Heavy infestations of this mite result in poor physical condition of the birds, including scabs and lower egg production. This mite does more damage than any other type of mite, and though it prefers the feathers below the vent and around the tail, northern fowl mites can be found on all parts of the body. They are extremely small, so you may need a magnifying glass to see them.

Common Chicken Mite

The common chicken mite feeds on birds at night and hides during the day. It is a blood-sucking mite, and when present in large numbers, the loss of blood and irritation may be enough to cause anemia in the bird. Egg production is also seriously reduced. This mite will survive in the poultry house up to five months after birds are removed. It can be transmitted by introducing infected chickens to your flock, by carrying it into the coop on boots and equipment, and possibly through wild birds. Treatment must include disinfecting the birds, coop, and equipment.

Scaly Leg Mite

These mites live under the scales on the feet and legs of chickens. They cause a thickening of the scales that makes it look like they are pointing directly outward, rather that lying flat on the leg. The mite spends its entire life cycle on the bird and is spread mainly by direct contact.

Depluming Mite

The depluming mite causes severe irritation by burrowing into the skin near the base of a feather, which frequently causes birds to cause internal bleeding. The intestinal lining wears away, and this may eventually result in death. If these parasites are present in large numbers, they are usually easy to find during an autopsy. Eggs may be difficult to find in droppings, however, because of their small size and the time of year the infection occurs. There isn't a treatment for capillaria, so you should attempt to control it using preventive measures. For example, additional vitamin A may help prevent this parasite from affecting your birds.

Tapeworms

Tapeworms are flat, ribbon-shaped worms that consist of many segments. They can be very small or several inches long, and the head is much smaller than the rest of the body. Since tapeworms may be very small, you have to look carefully to find them. You may need to open a portion of the intestine and place it in water to help find the tapeworms. When young birds have tapeworms, they get infections that result in low efficiency and slower growth. Young birds are more severely affected than older birds. Although several drugs have been used to remove tapeworms from chickens, some aren't that effective. Tapeworm infections are best controlled by preventing the birds from eating tapeworm eggs, but they can also be controlled by treating the birds regularly with fenbendazole or leviamisole.

Gapeworms

Gapeworms are round, red worms that attach themselves to a chicken's windpipe and cause the disease referred to as "gapes." The name of the disease describes the open-mouth-breathing characteristic of gapeworm-infected birds. Infected birds usually make grunt because they have difficulty breathing, and many die from suffocation. The worms can easily block the windpipe and are particularly harmful to young birds. You can best prevent gapeworms in your flock by administering a dewormer at fifteen- to thirty-day intervals or by giving your birds continuous low levels of a dewormer beginning fifteen days after the birds are placed in a pen with infected soil.

EXHIBITING CHICKENS

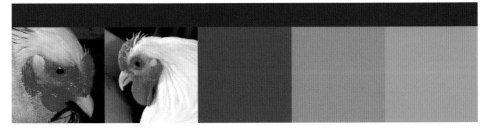

S howing chickens can be a lifelong project and passion. The culmination of many successful 4-H projects, poultry included, is exhibiting at the local, county, and state fairs. Raising your birds, caring for them daily, and learning more about the poultry-keeping hobby is something to be proud of and enjoyed. How better to show off your success than entering your birds at a fair or show? Your chickens will be judged and given a placing ribbon. The visitors who come through the fair barns catch the spirit of many aspects of rural America as they see young people taking care of their livestock projects. Seeing other birds helps you learn more about other breeds. It helps you to see where your birds match up in feather quality, size, and conformation in comparison to others. Fairs and shows are also a chance to meet other poultry enthusiasts, both young and old, and share your experiences.

Showing and exhibiting your birds can offer many rewards. This black Cochin cock has excellent feather and body condition and is a good type for a Cochin bantam. He garnered a first place in his class and went on to win Champion Bantam at his owner's county fair. *Chris Bell*

Banding your birds is a good and often necessary means of bird identification. There is a vast array of styles, sizes, and colors of leg bands. Practice careful application to ensure there is enough blood circulation to the shank and toes. Many shows will require your bird to have a band with a number on it for registration and to keep track of birds at the show. *Tara Kindschi*

a wide variety of styles, colors, and application methods. Be careful when applying them to young birds because the band may become too small and cause a circulation problem for the foot as the bird matures and the shank grows. Bands must be tight enough to avoid getting caught or falling off the foot but not too tight that the leg will swell. Always recheck a bird's band one to two days after applying as a safety measure. Leg bands can be removed and replaced with larger bands as the bird grows.

Selecting Show Birds

It is best to select your show birds before you enter a show. You will also have to decide how many birds you can afford to enter. Some shows charge per bird, others charge cage rental, and others require membership. Determine how much space you have to haul and transport your birds. Birds that are crowded into cages while traveling to a show do not look their best or place well. Any birds you take need to be washed and cage-tamed.

Large fowl Cochins of show quality are massive birds. The cock weighs an average of 11 pounds, and the hen will weigh 8 1/2 pounds. The birds take a full year or more to reach that mature size. *Kendall Babcock*

The number of birds you can afford to bring to shows may vary depending on the size, age, and sex of birds you choose to show. Make a list of the breeds you have, what ages, and what sex. Most county fairs only allow one entry per breed, age, and sex. If you raise a lot of black Wyandotte large fowl, you can only take your best cockerel, your best hen, your best pullet, and your best cock. APA-sanctioned shows allow you to enter as many birds as you like in each category, so if you have only black Wyandotte pullets, you could choose to take your top three and see which places the best.

As a second limiting factor, you should look closely at your birds. For shows,

Parts of Wing
1, Front. 2, Bow. 3, Bar. 4, Secondary. 5, Primaries. 6, Primary Coverts. 7, Wing Shoulder.

The wing comprises seven different parts. Learn all of them, especially the difference between the primary and secondary feathers, because this is a common showmanship mistake. Spreading the wings allows the judge to check for broken, twisted, or discolored feathers during show competition. *Reprinted from the* American Standard of Perfection *with permission from the APA*

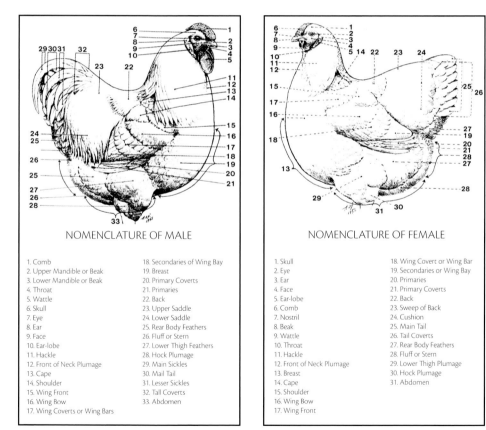

NOMENCLATURE OF MALE

1. Comb	18. Secondaries of Wing Bay
2. Upper Mandible or Beak	19. Breast
3. Lower Mandible or Beak	20. Primary Coverts
4. Throat	21. Primaries
5. Wattle	22. Back
6. Skull	23. Upper Saddle
7. Eye	24. Lower Saddle
8. Ear	25. Rear Body Feathers
9. Face	26. Fluff or Stern
10. Ear-lobe	27. Lower Thigh Feathers
11. Hackle	28. Hock Plumage
12. Front of Neck Plumage	29. Main Sickles
13. Cape	30. Mail Tail
14. Shoulder	31. Lesser Sickles
15. Wing Front	32. Tall Coverts
16. Wing Bow	33. Abdomen
17. Wing Coverts or Wing Bars	

NOMENCLATURE OF FEMALE

1. Skull	18. Wing Covert or Wing Bar
2. Eye	19. Secondaries or Wing Bay
3. Ear	20. Primaries
4. Face	21. Primary Coverts
5. Ear-lobe	22. Back
6. Comb	23. Sweep of Back
7. Nostril	24. Cushion
8. Beak	25. Main Tail
9. Wattle	26. Tail Coverts
10. Throat	27. Rear Body Feathers
11. Hackle	28. Fluff or Stern
12. Front of Neck Plumage	29. Lower Thigh Plumage
13. Breast	30. Hock Plumage
14. Cape	31. Abdomen
15. Shoulder	
16. Wing Bow	
17. Wing Front	

These illustrations are a great guide to help you learn all the external features on both male and female chickens. This is not only useful for showmanship and showing but for differentiating the sexes in the backyard flock as well. *Reprinted from the* American Standard of Perfection *with permission from the APA*

you must factor in breed type, individual disqualifications, and any disqualifications particular to a breed. Immediately take any birds off your list that have one of the following (if not a breed-specific trait):

- Deformed beaks
- Crooked or otherwise deformed backs
- A wing showing clipped flight or secondary feathers
- A split wing (a definite split between primary and secondary wing feathers)
- A slipped wing (unfolded and hanging down when the bird is standing)
- Twisted feathers in wing, sickles, or main tail feathers
- Main tail feathers entirely absent
- Wry tails (very crooked and tilt to one side)
- Squirrel tail (tail feathers that project forward over back)
- Lopped single comb
- Lopped rose comb (hanging to one side to obstruct sight)
- Split comb (blade of comb divided at right angles)
- Absence of spike in all rose comb varieties
- Side sprig or sprigs on all single comb varieties
- Crooked toes
- Webbing past the first knuckle on the toe (like a duck)
- Extra or missing toes
- Missing toenails
- Discolored ear lobe

Any birds that are taken off the list for a defect should also be first on your cull list. While the females may be fine for a laying flock, they shouldn't be used for breeding, since many of these traits are genetic and will therefore be passed to their offspring. The same is true with the males.

This La Fleche cock is the type of bird whose long, flowing tail requires a double coop at shows. A standard large fowl cage does not give him enough space to display or turn himself without possible tail feather breakage. Request a double coop on your entry blanks if needed and plan to pay twice the amount of the single-cage rate. *Levi Kindschi*

By now your list should be shorter, and it's time to narrow it down even more. There is no reason to waste your entry fee or preparation time on an inferior bird. Start looking at the individual birds and the following points:

- Birds must be well developed; young birds must be in their final plumage.
- Chickens should have the best body type for the breed.
- Birds should be uniform in color.
- Feathers must be well developed and not worn, broken, or ragged.
- Chickens should be healthy and free of disease.

This white Wyandotte bantam male shows excellent feather quality and cleanliness on his outspread wing. It is important to show only birds whose primary wing feathers are not missing or broken. Care in handling and cage removal is very important, since it can take three months or longer for these feathers to grow back.
DeAnn Richards

It is helpful to have someone assist you when selecting show birds. Sometimes a favorite bird remains on the list even though he or she has an obvious defect because you are too emotionally attached to see it. The same is true of a particular breed you may have purchased. All of your birds may have similar size and shape, but someone else can see that they are too far from the breed standard to exhibit. For example, you may have black Cochin large fowl hens that only weigh 5 pounds when the breed standard is 8 ½ pounds.

Once you have made your final selection of birds and sent in your entry form, take extra care with your birds until the show. The following items will help you maintain your birds until the time of the poultry show:

- Wash any extremely dirty areas of the bird.
- Check for external parasites and treat if needed.
- Place birds in cages or pens with clean bedding. Deeper bedding is recommended for feathered-leg and white varieties.
- Handle birds once or twice daily until the show. Getting the bird cage-tamed is very important. Judges don't like to handle birds that act wild and are difficult to hold. Judges spend less time while evaluating them and are left with a bad impression.
- Keep fresh feed and clean water available at all times. Adding a seed with higher oil content for a treat at this time can also add to the bird's overall feather sheen.
- Separate birds that are pecking on cagemates. Keeping each male you plan to exhibit in a separate pen and all the like-size females together in a larger pen often helps maintain feather quality and takes less room and fewer cages than keeping each bird separate.

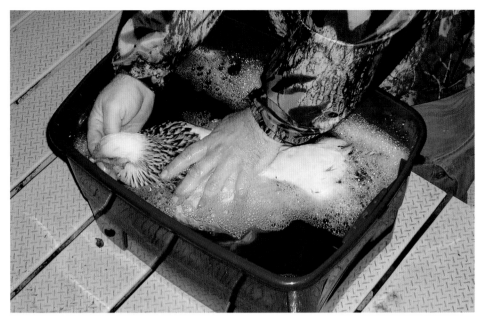

The white base of the Columbian pattern and the feathered legs and feet of a light Brahma hen benefit from washing before a show. This is the second tub where soap is applied and worked into the feathers. Extra attention is paid to the pea comb and wattle area, where dirt and feed are prone to buildup. *Shelly Sonsalla*

Here a black Australorp pullet and a white Leghorn bantam take their turns in the first tub (soaking area). Use extreme care when washing your birds. Chickens do not swim and can drown in a few inches of water if left unattended. *DeAnn Richards*

Wash Birds Before Shows

A chicken looks better clean. Some people only wash white or light-colored birds, but it really does help the feather quality on all chickens. Does a washed bird always place better than an unwashed bird? No, nothing cancels out a disqualification or defect, but a clean bird may mean the difference between a blue-ribbon (first place) and a champion chicken. Birds can and should be washed two to three days before a show. Depending on travel and time constraints, the very last day may not work or the weather may not cooperate. Chicken washing itself goes quite fast, but chicken drying takes some time! There are many commercial and homemade tools that you can use to wash your chicken. The following is a checklist of supplies to have and reasons to use them:

- A lot of warm water—very important for the bird's comfort and health
- Old towels or t-shirts—clean and absorbent
- Large sink or three large tubs—a laundry-type sink or tubs/pails large enough to immerse the entire bird
- Old toothbrush—extra scrub power for the feet and the comb area
- Nail clippers—plan to trim the toenails and beak
- Soap—nothing too harsh, and it needs to rinse out well
- Petroleum jelly or menthol rub—moisturize legs, comb, and wattles
- Warm sunshine—to aid in drying
- Blow dryer—if the sun isn't out or you have a loose-feathered breed
- Open, wire-type cage with deep bedding or towels on the floor

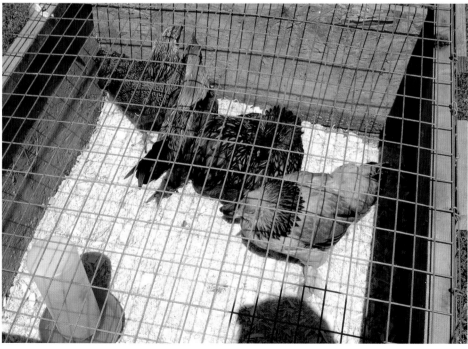

These four freshly washed bantams dry in the sun on a warm summer day. They have drinking water available and are checked regularly for comfort. Note how dry the close-feathered Modern Game is compared to the thicker fluff on the bantam buff Brahma pullet. *Kelly Damaschke*

If you have several chickens to wash, start with the breed that has the most feathers, such as the Cochins or Brahmas. They will need the longest time to dry. Save your hard-feathered breeds, such as Malays and Cornish, as the last to be washed.

The following method described is for those with access to a large sink. If using the three-tub method, fill your bucket with clean, warm water for steps one through three. Switch to a second bucket filled with warm, soapy water for steps four and five, and use a third bucket of clean, warm water for steps seven through ten.

> Birds can and should be washed two to three days before a show. Depending on travel and time constraints, the last day before a show may not work or the weather may not cooperate. Chicken washing itself goes quite fast, but chicken drying takes some time!

Have an extra set of hands ready if you need help keeping the bird in the water or to hand you supplies. You will need to have at least one of your hands on the bird at all times, and that can be tricky for beginners and experts alike.

Bathing a Chicken

Step 1: Fill the sink with warm water. The temperature should be the same as you would prefer for bath water. Put your arm in the water, and if it feels too hot or cold for you, it is the wrong temperature for the chicken.

Step 2: Hold the bird securely with both hands over the wing and body and completely immerse its body, including the head, for three seconds. Raise the bird so its head is out of the water so it can breathe. Then hold the bird against the side of the sink with one hand to keep the bird secure and work the water past the feathers to the skin with your other hand. The bird's natural oils will resist water at first, so you must force the water past the outer feathers to the fluff and skin.

Pre-wash any extremely dirty areas on your chicken in the soap tub before wetting the entire bird. This saves on the time that the bird will be completely soaked and helps prevent the bird from getting chilled. An extra set of hands is helpful. One person can hold the bird, and the other person can do the rubbing, washing, and rinsing. *Jerilyn Johnson*

Step 3: Switch hands and the side of sink you are on to work water onto the other side of the chicken's body.

Step 4: Take some of the soap, such as a liquid shampoo or dish soap, and spread a marble-sized amount onto your free palm.

Step 5: Gently rub the soap into the feathers, and always rub in the direction the feathers grow. Work up a lather on the body section from hackle to tail. Only use more soap if you need to for feather-footed breeds or for an extremely dirty vent area. Soap removes the natural oils from the feathers, along with any dirt, so use soap sparingly to keep the feathers from getting brittle.

Step 6: Take your toothbrush and thoroughly clean around the eyes, nostrils, wattles, and comb.

Step 7: While still soaped, change your hold on the bird so you can concentrate on the shanks, toes, and nails. Use the toothbrush to clean every scale. A bird with feathered legs may need more soap to get encrusted grime out of those feathers. Always use the toothbrush in the same direction the feathers grow to avoid breakage.

Step 8: Drain the water from the sink. Run your hand from the bird's hackles to its tail, gently squeezing out all the soap and water that you can.

Step 9: Refill the sink with clean, warm water.

A kiddie swimming pool of sun-warmed water is used as a final rinse tank for a white Cochin frizzle bantam cockerel. His small size and calm demeanor allows the girl to hold him with one hand and rinse with the other. *Kelly Damaschke*

Step 10: Repeat Step 1 and work the clean water into the same fluff and feathers to remove all soap residue. Keep rinsing the bird for five minutes after you think you have it all out. If in doubt, or if the water still seems soapy, empty the sink and rinse again.

Step 11: Once the bird is fully rinsed, run your hand from its hackles to tail and gently squeeze out all the water you can. Also run down the breast area and the back fluff and vent area to remove as much water as you can.

Step 12: Remove the chicken from the sink area.

Step 13: Use a towel and drape it over the bird's back. Carefully wrap the ends under the breast and feet to form a tube with the chicken secure on its side.

Step 14: Get your nail clippers and a chair. Sit with the bird wrapped on your lap. Look at the beak and even out the top and lower mandibles, if needed. Always reform the beak's shape into a natural "V." An overbite keeps a bird from eating and sorting food and should even be trimmed on non-show birds.

Step 15: Unwrap the bird enough to see both legs and check all toenail lengths. Trim them if they are too long. When in doubt, take tiny snips and watch for the bird's reaction. Stop trimming if you draw blood or see pink in the nail. If they jerk like it hurts or you see a bloody end on the nail, it is short enough. Most breeds under one year of age and those birds that free-range generally don't require nail-trimming. Older birds, birds raised

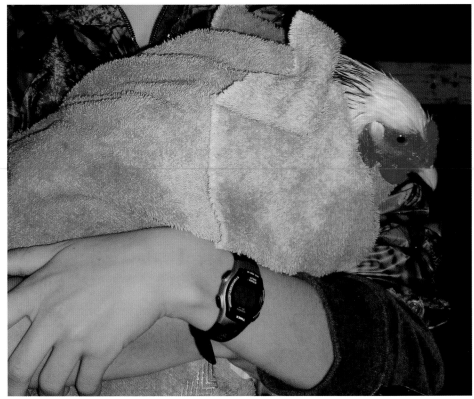

Wrapping a chicken's body in a towel for several minutes after the final rinse allows excess water to be absorbed without damaging any feathers. Keeping the wings and feet tucked into the towel will give you more control of the chicken.
Shelly Sonsalla

A white Leghorn cock bantam is ready for his bath. His upper beak is overgrown and needs a trim with a small nail clipper. This is quite common in birds over one year of age. Overgrown beaks should be trimmed, not only for show purposes, but also to allow the bird to have an easier time when eating. *DeAnn Richards*

on wire flooring, and some of the feather-footed breeds grow longer nails that must be trimmed for showing and for the bird's daily comfort.

Step 16: Remove the towel and carefully check the bird. Is it shaking or huddled? If it is and the weather is warm and sunny, place the bird in a prepared wire cage in the sunlight and check it every ten to fifteen minutes. If there is no sunlight or it is cool or rainy, get out your blow dryer.

Step 17: Blow dry the chicken using a medium speed and medium heat setting. The idea is to dry and warm the bird without breaking or changing the direction of the feathers. If your hand gets too hot under the dryer, it is also too hot for the bird. Start on the breast and fluff areas and work your way up. Lift the wings and do the underside and the body. Keep turning and working different spots as you go.

Step 18: Do not completely dry the bird with a blow dryer. Just dry it to the point where feathers start to fluff back on their own.

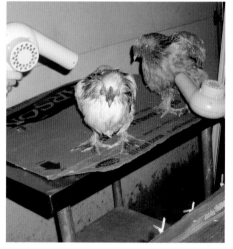

Hair dryers work well on feathers. Use medium to low heat and speed settings and go over the entire body, remembering to get under the wings. Plan to spend a half-hour blow-drying each bird. *Shelly Sonsalla*

Step 19: If the bird is almost dry, not shaking or huddled, and is attempting to shake like a dog, you have it dry and comfortable enough to place it in the prepared cage in an area away from drafts.

This buff Wyandotte hen has been thoroughly washed and dried to the point of damp. With warmth from the sun or an added heat lamp, she will work on fluffing and arranging all of her clean feathers and looking her best for a show in the next few days. *DeAnn Richards*

Step 20: You are almost done. Continue checking the bird in the cage until you are sure it is warm enough and dry. At that point, take the bird out and apply a thin coating of petroleum jelly or menthol rub to the shanks on clean-leg breeds and the comb and wattles on all breeds. This will condition the comb and feet to look extra clean and healthy. Make sure you don't get any on the clean feathers.

Step 21: Return the washed, clipped, and dried bird to a clean pen or cage until it is time to load for the show.

It is normal and okay for a chicken to ruffle and work the feathers over with its beak. The bird will do the best job of fixing and straightening all those clean feathers. Remember that birds don't swim and can drown if left unattended in the water. Birds that get very chilled in cold water or are not dried properly may go into shock and die.

Show Packing

You will need to take your birds of course, but what else? Talk to show sponsors and carefully read the entry form. Make sure you have the following items.

Transport Cages

Getting your birds to the show requires some type of cage or carrier. It can be the same flat-bottomed cage you used at washing time, it can be a wooden chicken box designed for your size of birds with ventilation holes and handles for carrying, or it can be a pet carrier usually used for cats or dogs. Use care when placing birds in the cage or carrier, and never crowd too many in one space to prevent feathers from being damaged.

Show Caging

Show caging is usually supplied in the appropriate size for your entry; there are cages made just for bantams and for large fowl. Most are put on top of a piece of plywood or a wooden board for a base. If you have a very large male bird with a flowing tail, you may think about asking for a double coop, which will be listed on the entry form. You will also have to pay a double entry fee for that bird.

Some small school fairs may ask you to supply your own cage. If that is the case, try to use cages that are easy for the judge to access, keep the bird visible from all sides, and have a flat bottom to let the bird stand at its best.

A custom-made caging system fits multiple uses. Here it is being used to display birds for sale at a chicken swap. It can be unstacked and turned sideways to fit inside a truck topper and used for hauling birds to shows. It is nicely sized for bantam pairs. *Tara Kindschi*

Feed

Some shows supply feed and some do not. One-day shows normally don't. If you live nearby and the birds will only be at the show for a few hours, feed is not necessary. At a county fair or two-day show, you will need to be prepared to feed your bird daily. Some exhibitors don't like the hassle of bringing feed and use the show feed if supplied. Others like their birds to have the same food all the time and bring it along whether the show supplies it or not. Read the entry form so you know your options and decide what you want to do beforehand. You will always be required to fill your own feed and water cups at least daily.

Feed and Water Containers

All standard cages have a hanger to hold a small cup for water. Some also have a hanger for a feed cup. Check to see if the cups will be provided or if you need to bring your own. Supply houses also sell bigger containers that hang on the cage, as well as an apparatus that converts a 20-ounce bottle to a waterer. Keep in mind that whatever you choose, it shouldn't interfere with the judge's viewing of the bird or the bird's movements.

Bedding

Pine shavings are best. Check into whether the show supplies them or if you need to bring your own. Bedding should be changed or freshened daily at multi-day shows to keep your bird clean and on solid footing.

Show Box

There are several items you will need to have for last-minute prep of your birds before judging. A small toolbox or fishing tackle box works well. Plan to stock it with the following items:

- Extra leg or wing bands
- Baby wipes
- Cotton swabs
- Petroleum jelly or menthol rub
- Silk handkerchief
- Baby or olive oil
- Nail clippers
- Tape
- Copy of your entry form
- Health papers the show requires

Volunteer

Hosting and organizing a poultry show,

Chicken exhibitors often use show boxes to help organize the process for packing and getting birds ready before a show. This is also a place to put extra copies of health papers and show entry forms. *Tara Kindschi*

whether for fifty birds at a county fair or five thousand birds at a national meet, takes a lot of work and effort. All the work is usually done by volunteers who love poultry. You are showing for the same reasons. You and your family can help support the show through volunteering for a multitude of tasks including the following:

Cage setup—this is a very labor-intensive project usually done the weekend before a big show.

Bedding cages—this is done after the cages are set up and is a good job for the younger poultry enthusiast.

Clerking—these volunteers keep track of the judging. This also allows you to spend time with a judge and pick up some extra tips about breeds and show preparation.

Food stand—this is the main fundraiser for shows, and kitchen help is always needed for a few hours during the show.

Cage tear-down—this starts as soon as the birds are released from the show and has to go on until it's complete. The more volunteers, the faster the job is done.

Show Expectations

If you've never been present during judging at a county fair or attended an APA-sanctioned show, it may all seem a bit fast-paced and confusing. Read the check-in times and be there at the beginning. Plan extra time for the following:

- Finding the show grounds.
- Parking. Poultry shows are popular places at entry time, and parking can be at a premium.
- Checking in at the registration table to get your exhibitor number.
- Having birds examined at check-in by a show official for mites or signs of poor health.
- Finding and possibly having to bed your cages.
- Putting feed and water cups into each cage.
- Cleaning any birds that got dirty on the trip.

How birds are organized at local and state fairs varies greatly. At some fairs all birds

Planning ahead and being organized the morning of a fast-paced one-day show is very important. Here, the birds are cooped in, there is water in their cups, their tags are correct, and the participant is enjoying himself. All that is left to do is to remove the boxes and cages used for transporting the birds and supplies. *Tara Kindschi*

may be grouped together in a spot and then taken into a show ring for judging. Other fairs arrange the birds by classes, breeds, and varieties. Cage space at some county and state fairs may be limited, and you may have to coop the male and female of the same breed together if you entered both. Be flexible and work with show officials. Don't ask for last-minute substitutions. If a bird you entered is sick or doesn't look right and you choose not to bring it, that is fine, but don't plan to bring another bird in its place unless it is the exact same variety, age, and sex.

APA shows are a bit more standardized. Cages will be prearranged by variety, breed, age, and sex. All of your entries will not be in one spot. You will learn your exhibitor number when you check in at the show table and then look for that number on the cards attached to the cages in the areas for varieties you entered. Junior show entries are usually in a different spot than the birds entered in the open show. The cage card must exactly match the bird you put in it, since that card is what the judge will go by. If the card says pullet and you put a cockerel in that cage, the

bird will be disqualified as the wrong sex for the class. A copy of your show entry can help you verify if there are any mistakes when you get to the show. The show clerk has entered and made cards for many birds (sometimes thousands), and mistakes happen. Be patient and let a show official know the problem long before judging starts so there is plenty of time to try and correct the situation. Nothing can be done after a bird is judged.

This large fowl, black Langshan pullet has been handled regularly. She stands calmly and correctly while the judge examines her. A judge can better determine a bird's qualities if the bird is not flapping, crouching, or struggling while being handled. *Jerilyn Johnson*

Judges at large shows work through lines of birds that are cooped according to variety and age. The top birds go on to compete within their breed and then class. The top birds of the show are moved into a line of coops called "Champion Row." *Tara Kindschi*

This silver-laced Wyandotte cock is ready for the judge's inspection. The judge will use the General Scale of Points to rate this bird on sixteen different criteria, with a perfect bird scoring a possible one hundred. *DeAnn Richards*

Birds at county and state fairs are judged two different ways: face-to-face or in-line. Face-to-face is when each exhibitor stands with his or her bird in its respective class. Usually a row of cages is set up, and you bring your bird and put it into the cage when your class is called. The judge reviews all the entries and handles each bird one at a time. Birds are then placed using the scale of points found in the *American Standard of Perfection*. Most judges will give an oral critique to the bird owners and within listening range of anyone who may be watching.

In-line judging at fairs involves the judge having total privacy to look at each class of entries. Any comments that he or she has about a bird are written on the cage card. The birds are arranged by class, variety, sex, and age, and the judging moves down the line of cages.

The Danish placing system is used at most fairs. Only a certain percentage of first-place ribbons can be given, a certain number of second-place ribbons, and so on through fourth place. Every bird entered receives a placing and corresponding ribbon or award sticker. The top birds are reviewed again to compete for any awards, such as Best American Class, Champion Bantam, and Reserve Champion of Show. The judging itself may take several hours depending on how many judges there are and how many birds there are to be viewed.

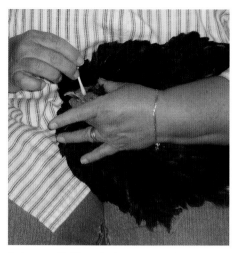

Sit down and hold your bird on your lap with one arm and use your other hand to apply petroleum jelly or menthol rub properly to your chicken's comb and wattles for that final show finish. Using a cotton swab instead of your finger ensures you won't over-apply into the feathers. *Tara Kindschi*

This head shot of a barred Plymouth Rock pullet shows a nice single comb that has been moisturized for that extra healthy sheen. Her cage is well bedded and clean of any extra droppings and is ready for the judge. *Levi Kindschi*

There are many other tips to give your bird a final, polished look. Experiment with any of the following tips at home first to get comfortable doing them and to make sure they make your particular bird look better.

APA-sanctioned shows are judged in-line. Winners of the Best and Reserve of Variety awards are named, and the birds go on to compete for Best and Reserve of Breed. Next come the awards for Best and Reserve of Class, then the Champion and Reserve of each division, and finally Champion of Show.

Judging Preparation

Take a few minutes to look over every bird you have entered before judging begins. Check for any feathers that look ruffled or out of place and fix them. Make sure the bedding is dry and clean; remove any clumps of manure. Check the bird's feet and vent areas for any manure and remove it with a baby wipe as needed.

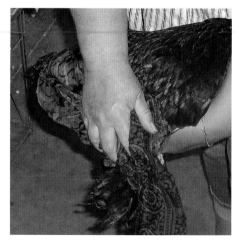

Giving your show entries a finished appearance can help your chickens place better at the show. Running a pure silk scarf over the entire body of a solid-black chicken is a technique used to bring out that extra green sheen of feathers in excellent condition. *Tara Kindschi*

A black bird may benefit from lightly running a pure silk handkerchief run over its body. It really brings out that beetle-green sheen just before judging.

A thin coat of petroleum jelly or menthol rubbed on the combs, feet, and wattles adds a finishing touch. Don't do this to the shanks on feather-leg breeds because it will dirty the leg feathers. The menthol brings up the red color, while straight petroleum jelly adds a glossy sheen.

You can moisturize the bottom of a bird's feet with olive oil or baby oil for a richer, healthy-looking skin. Use your body and one arm to nestle the bird upside down and apply the oil. This is also a good position for trimming overgrown toenails. *Tara Kindschi*

Apply baby oil or olive oil to the bottom of the feet to make the skin look extra rich and healthy.

You will hear of or see many other techniques used to enhance a bird's appearance for a show. Some may not be legal or in the best interest of your bird. Altering a feather's shape or changing the natural color of any section of a feather is prohibited at all shows. Cutting or trimming a comb to remove side springs is a disqualification. Before you try any new techniques, ask yourself if this is something you would want done to your body. If the answer is no, don't do it to your bird.

Showmanship

Another increasingly popular part of junior poultry showing is showmanship. It is usually treated as a competition at poultry shows, with prizes, and is divided into different age groups that may include a beginner, junior, intermediate, and senior division set by age or years of experience showing poultry.

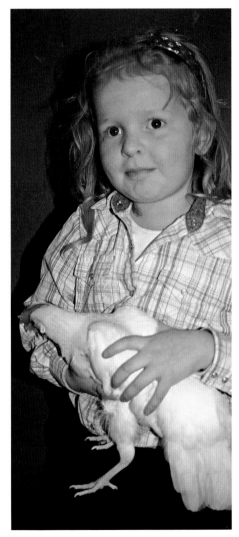

Young adults can participate in showmanship at different skill levels. Here a beginner exhibitor proudly displays her very clean and calm white Leghorn bantam hen. The questions and level of handling skill become more challenging as the competitor ages. *DeAnn Richards*

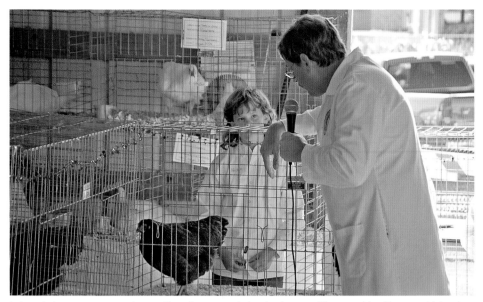

Judges ask the contestants questions and listen for answers during the showmanship competition. Showmanship involves specific knowledge and handling of a bird, plus general poultry knowledge, and it is graded using a one-hundred-point system. There are usually categories for junior, intermediate, and senior based on age, grade in school, or years of showing. *Corallina Breuer*

Showmanship can be most easily defined as the ability to share your knowledge of poultry in general and of a specific breed with a judge. For showmanship, you need to have knowledge of all poultry, including large fowl and bantam chickens, ducks, geese, and turkeys. You should present yourself in a professional manner with recommended clothing; a clean, manageable bird; and a lot of knowledge.

What You Should Wear

Recommended showmanship clothing includes a white show coat over a plain, button-down collared shirt; dark pants; and sensible shoes. Your clothing should not detract the judge's eye from the bird toward you. Do not wear bright T-shirts with bold lettering, patterned shorts, or flip-flops. Do not chew gum during your showmanship interview.

What You Need to Know

Your showmanship skills are based on two basic components: your poultry knowledge

Numerous young adults participate in the showmanship contests at shows sanctioned by the APA and ABA. Exhibitors range in age from five to nineteen years old. Contestants informally hold fun quizzing sessions before the real competition to learn more about poultry in general, poultry breeds, and showmanship pointers. *Tara Kindschi*

and your ability to handle a bird correctly. The bird you choose to demonstrate your

The judge and a junior showmanship contestant will discuss a bird during a competition. Not only will exhibitors be asked to explain the parts of a bird, its breed, and other qualities, but they'll also answer general poultry questions that may pertain to ducks, turkeys, and geese. *Patti Delaney-Ruhland*

showmanship skills is important. You should choose a breed that is in the *American Standard of Perfection*. It should be a breed that you know about or want to learn a lot about by memorizing the descriptions of that breed and variety in the *American Standard of Perfection*, including comb type, weights by sex, disqualifications, origins of the breed, and all recognized varieties. Take special note of anything unique in the breed. Does it have fifth toes? Is it recognized in different comb types? Is it a bantam-only breed or does it have a large fowl counterpart? Have an adult, your project leader, or a fellow youth poultry enthusiast quiz you on the breed. Practice until you know all the details and are comfortable speaking about them.

When speaking with the judge, make sure you speak loud enough and slow enough to be clearly understood by the judge. This seems logical, but people tend to talk faster and quieter when nervous. The judge wants to hear what you have to say.

Make sure you can correctly answer the following twenty questions. You may or may not be asked all of these exact questions, but you will have to know similar information. Asking yourself these questions is great

practice to get you prepared for showmanship. When you are comfortable with all these questions and the answers, make up your own questions and practice with someone to test your knowledge further. If you don't know an answer to a question, be honest with the judge and say you do not know. If this happens, make sure you learn the correct answer so that you are prepared for the next show.

1. What ingredients are used to make commercially balanced poultry feeds?
2. What is a chicken's crop used for?
3. Name and show at least five body parts of your bird.
4. How long does a chicken egg take to incubate?
5. What are mites? Where would you most likely find them on your bird? How do you treat them?
6. Name a breed of chicken with five toes.
7. Name a breed that is only recognized in bantam.
8. Name a breed of bird with a rose comb.
9. What is a female chicken less than one year of age called?
10. Generally, if a hen lays white eggs, what color is her earlobe?
11. Show where a sex feather would be found on a bird.
12. What is a side sprig?
13. What is a male more than one year old called?
14. Name a variety of chicken where the male has a different color pattern than the female.
15. Name a breed of chicken in which a lopped single comb in the hen is required.
16. What is the difference between a pullet and a hen?
17. Do you need a rooster for a hen to lay eggs?
18. What does the term "broody" refer to?
19. Name a disqualification in a white Leghorn cock.
20. Name a breed with a crest.

Your Bird Choice

The actual bird you choose for showmanship should have no defects or disqualifications. It should be old enough to have its final adult plumage. The chicken should be calm and used to being handled. This will make your showmanship demonstration go smoother and make the judge's job easier.

Correct Handling

Correctly taking a bird out of a cage or carrier is important at all times, not just for showmanship. A simple rule to remember is, "Always bring the bird out of the cage in the direction that its feathers grow." Broken feathers, especially in the wings, detract from the bird's score when being judged. A feather may take as long as two to three months to grow back completely. Follow these steps to remove a bird correctly and then reverse the steps to put a bird back in a cage.

Correctly holding and handling a large breed can be a challenge for younger exhibitors. Working with chickens every day when they are chicks and juveniles will help keep them calm, tame, and manageable. This black Langshan pullet feels comfortable and secure and is not struggling or flapping her wings. *Kendall Babcock*

- Move in a slow, calm manner. Don't rush yourself or the bird.
- Stand directly in front of the cage and use your body to block any possible bird escapes.
- Put both hands and arms into the cage and move in on the bird slowly. You want to aim both hands for the body and grasp it over the wings.
- At this point, don't worry about which direction the bird is facing. It can easily be turned later, after you have it secure in your hands.
- Grip the bird firmly with one hand covering each wing, take the bulk of the body in your hands, and lift it up just enough so the feet are off the ground.
- Use your wrists to turn the bird so the head faces the cage door. If you have to turn it so far that you have to switch hands on each side of the body, do so now.

- Draw the bird out of the cage and up into the cradle of your arms.
- Use your body and one hand to hold the bird and proceed to get your hands in the body hold described below. This body hold is also the best way to carry a bird, with the bird's weight resting on your arm.

Holding a bird correctly takes practice. Start by splitting the fingers on your non-dominant hand (left hand if you are a right-handed person) and keep your middle and ring fingers straight between the bird's legs. Use your first and pinky fingers to grip around each leg. In this position the bird is secure, and you can use your palm and thumb to balance the bird's weight. A bird held like this feels secure and will not struggle or flap its wings. You can use your other hand on the bird's back and wings and your arm and body to stabilize and keep

Many trophies and awards are given at poultry shows for both the junior and open divisions of exhibitors. A part of good sportsmanship is always remembering to congratulate the winner. If you are the winner, always write a formal thank-you note to the sponsor of your trophy or award. *Tara Kindschi*

the wings down, if needed. When set, you can draw the bird away from your body and rotate your wrist to position the bird either facing forward or back. It is best to present it facing forward to the judge. In this position, you or the judge can clearly see all of the bird, spread its wings to examine the feathers, or tip it on its side or back to look at breast and vent areas. The act of getting the bird out of the cage, into your hold, and presented to the judge in a quiet smooth process takes practice for you and the bird. Younger presenters and those with a small stature may benefit greatly from choosing a bantam breed, since the sheer weight of a large bird and its leg thickness can become almost impossible to grip and support in small hands. Breeds like Silkies and Cochin are calmer in nature and may be quicker to train and easier to handle. Females tend to be quieter and less likely to peck or get aggressive during cage removal.

Sportsmanship

Life is about more than who won and who lost. What did you learn along the way? How did you help others to learn? Was it an enjoyable experience? Those are the questions that you need to ask and continually strive to achieve. Remember the following points for being a good sport:

- Always congratulate the winner.
- Learn something from every experience—good or bad.
- Don't argue with a judge or show official.
- Treat your birds with kindness and consideration for their entire lives.

Market Classes

Market class is a very unique niche within the poultry project at some county and state fairs. The exhibits in these classes are the

A clean and dry layer of wood shavings keeps this pen of white Cornish-cross pullets very clean and prevents breast blisters. Blisters are quite common in broilers, since they spend so much of their day resting on the ground. Broilers have unique feed requirements and should not be raised with other chickens, such as layers or bantams. *USDA*

culmination of a very rewarding, short-term project from its start as a chick to a finished live-meat product. The class divisions vary by fair but usually include a separate broiler and roaster division. Pairs of same-sex birds form a pen, and the pen is judged as a set. The pen of birds is judged on several criteria, including the following:

- Individual conformation, including no defects or disqualifications, such as bent toes, crooked combs, breast blisters, or split wings
- Weight as close to ideal for the class
- Uniformity within the pair in weight and body shape
- Cleanliness

Depending on the fair, the top-placing birds in these divisions are eligible to sell in a meat sale, with local businesses supporting the youth projects by bidding for these animals at an auction. Other animal projects typically represented at the meat sale include beef, swine, and sheep.

Helpful Tips for Cornish-Cross Meat Birds

Order straight-run chicks. The males and females grow at different rates, and this will give you two size options from which to choose.

These birds do best when raised on grass in a movable pen, also referred to as a chicken tractor. Move to fresh grass daily to keep the birds clean, give them fresh greens, and avoid bad legs by keeping them from slippery conditions.

These birds don't handle heat well. Supply a fan for the birds on hot days and provide plenty of shade and fresh drinking water.

Helpful Tips for a Successful Sale

Contact local businesses before the sale in person or via a typed letter explaining who you are, what your project involves, and how you would use any award money.

- Enter the ring dressed for showmanship and have your bird or birds clean and looking their best.
- Smile during the auction.
- Personally thank your buyer after the sale.
- Send a formal thank-you note to the business after the sale.

The commercial Cornish crosses used for market classes grow extremely fast, and a 5- to 6-pound bird can be achieved in as little as six weeks, with ten weeks giving you an 8-plus-pound bird when managed properly. These chicks are predominately white-feathered with yellow skin and are sold through hatcheries under many names, such as Jumbo Cross, Super Grower, and Cornish X. Even as chicks, they have different feeding and space requirements than other chickens. Their extremely fast growth rate must be regulated by providing feed for only part of the day, unlike free-choice for other chicks. They are slow moving, and although they are bigger than other chicks, they will be the first to be picked on if you attempt to raise them together with other breeds. Plan a completely separate area for these broiler/roaster chicks and have a grow-out pen designed for their special needs.

A successful poultry project show day for these sisters leaves both birds and contestants happy and content. Both birds are good examples of their bantam varieties with no defects or disqualifications, and both were calm and easily managed during showmanship.
Kelly Damaschke

Chapter 8

HELP AND ADVICE

You may have questions about your poultry project. There are a number of helpful resources you can call on to answer your questions and provide advice.

County Agricultural Extension Services

The agricultural extension service is generally located in your county seat. A staff of experts in various agricultural and 4-H areas is available to help with answers to questions and solutions to problems. They provide useful, practical, and research-based information to agricultural producers, small business owners, young people, consumers, and others who live in rural areas and communities of all sizes.

Here is a collection of magazines and books to help anyone learn more about chicken raising and poultry keeping in general. These can be useful guides to the beginner or long-time flock owner. Most poultry enthusiasts enjoy sharing their knowledge through articles and photographs. *Tara Kindschi*

There are many printed resources for general poultry knowledge and breed specifics. Here twins enjoy learning more from the *American Standard of Perfection* as they await their turn at showmanship at a local fair. *DeAnn Richards*

4-H Programs

Over six million youth participate in 4-H programs throughout the United States. Most 4-H programs center around three areas: leadership, citizenship, and life skills.

There are projects in just about any topic you would like to explore. 4-H members learn life skills by making decisions and setting goals, building teamwork, learning to relate to others, and learning by doing. While ages for 4-H membership vary by state, typically young people ages eight through eighteen can participate. Clubs for 4-H members hold meetings, elect officers, create exhibits, and provide opportunities for public speaking and participation in events like the county fair, workshops, and recreational activities with other clubs. One of the most valuable skills you learn in 4-H is to keep a yearly project record book where you log in your projects and experiences throughout the year.

The 4-H program is a part of the Cooperative Extension System, a non-profit program operated through each state's land-grant university. The extension system's staff oversees 4-H offices in most counties of each state. Your local club may have a poultry leader, and there is usually also a county-wide poultry project leader or a poultry superintendent for the fair. 4-H offers many poultry-related programs and activities including shows, judging teams, and project clubs.

FFA Chapters

Many school districts have an FFA chapter. The chapter advisor is usually an agricultural educator at the high school level. He or she may have firsthand knowledge of poultry. If not, he or she will have access to a wide network of information and connections to other FFA members who specialize in poultry. Some schools have poultry-judging teams that compete in regional and state competitions.

GLOSSARY

ABA: American Bantam Association

abdomen: Area between the pubic bones and keel.

air cell: Air space in the end of an egg, usually the larger end.

American: Class of large fowl chickens developed in North America that includes Rocks, Delawares, Rhode Islands, Chanteclers, and Buckeyes.

American Standard of Perfection: A comprehensive guide that is the official poultry breed standard in North America; published by the American Poultry Association (APA).

anatomy: The structural systems of a bird; includes skeleton, muscles, digestive tract, and more.

AOSB (Any Other Standard Breed): Class of large fowl chickens that includes Game, Turken, Phoenix, and Oriental breeds.

APA: American Poultry Association

axial feather: The short feather growing between the primary and secondary feathers of the wing.

back: The top section of the body from base of neck to base of tail; includes the cape and saddle.

banding: Putting a tag or band with letters or numbers on a leg or wing to identify one bird from another.

This young chick has a wing band. Wing bands are one way to identify your birds. The bands can be applied at a very young age and last throughout the bird's life. They are often hidden in the wing feathers on adult birds but can easily be found. *USDA*

This close-up of a wing shows the barred coloring on a male bird. Females in barred varieties have more subtle black versus white stripes, since females have only one barring gene where males have two. *Corallina Breuer*

bantam: A miniature chicken that may be as small as one-fourth the size of its large fowl counterpart.

barbicel: Tiny hook that holds the feather's web together (except in the Silkie breed).

barring: Alternate markings of two distinct colors on a feather.

bay: Light golden brown in color.

beak: The horny formation projecting from the head that consists of an upper and lower mandible.

beard: A cluster of feathers growing from the upper throat of some breeds and found only in combination with muffs.

beginner: Usually an age or grade division for starting show participants.

blade: The lower, smooth part of a single comb or the portion of the single comb to the rear of the last point of the male bird.

blister: Enlarged, discolored area on the breast or keel bone often seen in heavy market birds.

blood spot: Blood in an egg caused when a small blood vessel breaks at ovulation.

bloom: Peak condition of an exhibition bird.

blowout: Vent damage caused by laying an oversized egg.

blue: A slate gray feather color.

booted: Chickens that have feathers on their legs, such as the Sultan breed.

breast: The forward portion of the underside of the body from the point where the neck joins the body to the point directly between the legs.

mulberry: The deep purplish-red color of combs and wattles on some breeds, such as Silkies.

neck: Attaches the head to the body; length varies by breed.

necropsy: Determining the cause of death in poultry.

nest box: A man-made box where hens lay their eggs.

nostril: The outside opening on the upper mandible of the beak used for breathing.

NPIP: National Poultry Improvement Plan. A USDA program directed at the control and elimination of poultry diseases that can be transmitted through the reproductive process.

oyster shell: Used as a source of extra calcium for laying hens.

pasting: Loose droppings stuck to the vent area where manure is expelled. Often seen in young, stressed chicks.

pencilled: Crosswise lines or bars on feathers that form a pattern.

pendulous crop: A swollen crop, visible hanging over the breast area, that contains foul-smelling fluid, feed, and litter; also called drop crop.

pipped: A chick that has successfully broken a hole in the egg's shell in the hatching process.

plumage: The collection of feathers that covers the entire body of a bird.

poultry: A general term used for all domestic fowl.

points: The tips on a single comb.

predator: An animal that hunts another for food.

premises registration: An effort to identify all the locations in the United States where livestock and poultry are raised or housed. This is a first step in improving animal disease response. Registration of the area you keep your flock is required in some states. Before keeping any poultry, check with your state's department of agriculture to see if you are required to register the premises where your birds are housed.

primary feather: The long, stiff feathers of the wing; also called flight feathers.

protein: A nutritional requirement for chickens. The percentage of protein available in commercially prepared feeds is listed on the label—the source of protein is usually soybeans.

pubic bones: Portions of the hip bones that form part of the pelvis; used to help judge the productivity of laying hens.

purebred: A breed when mated with the same breed always produces like offspring.

pullet: A female chicken under one year of age.

ration: A nutritionally balanced feed.

resistance: Immunity to infection.

roach back: A deformed, hunched back; a disqualification for showing.

roost: A place, usually elevated, where a chicken sleeps.

rooster: A generic term for any male chicken. The terms *cock* and *cockerel* are used in exhibition vocabulary.

roaster: Market chickens between three and five months old. They are larger and older than broilers.

rumpless: A genetic trait in some chicken breeds where they have no tail feathers.

saddle: The rear portion on the back of a chicken that extends to the tail in a male fowl. It can also refer to an apron used on hens to protect their back feathers when exposed to over-mating.

salmon: A color that is a medium shade of red ochre.

sanitize: To clean and disinfect in order to kill germs and bacteria.

scales: Thin, horny growths that completely cover the shanks and top of the toes.

scaly leg: A condition on the shanks and toes of a fowl caused by a burrowing mite.

secondary feather: The long, stiff feathers growing from the middle wing segment; next to the primary feathers.

senior: An age or grade grouping for advanced exhibitors at shows.

sex feathers: Feathers in the hackle, back, saddle, and sickle that end in points in the male and are round in the female.

shaft: Part of the feather where the barbs are attached.

shank: The part of a chicken's leg between the claw and the first joint.

showmanship: A show competition that involves presenting your bird and your knowledge of it to a judge.

sickles: The long, curved rooster tail feathers.

side sprig: A point or projection from the side of a single comb; a disqualification in all single-comb breeds.

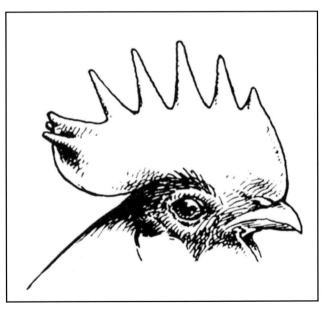

Side sprigs can occur on any area of the comb. A side sprig is a disqualification in both males and females; look carefully before entering a bird in a show or using it for breeding stock. It is illegal to remove a side sprig. *Reprinted from the* American Standard of Perfection *with permission from the APA*

A close-up of this cock's foot shows the spur on its inner shank. A spur on a female chicken is a disqualification. Spurs, in addition to sex feathers, and an enlarged comb or wattles all are indicators of a male bird.
Kendall Babcock

spent: A hen that no longer lays well.

spike: The round extension found at the end of a rose comb.

splash: A color pattern that results from matings involving blue genetics.

spraddle leg: A condition often observed in chicks where legs splay (spread or turn out) from the body rather than being upright under the body; often caused by slippery footing.

spur: A horny projection on each lower leg of adult male birds; a disqualification on a hen.

squirrel tail: A tail that has more than a ninety-degree angle.

straight-run: Selling unsexed chicks. It means "as hatched," and the percentage of male to female can vary greatly.

stub: Feathers located on the shank or toe of a clean-legged chicken.

trachea: Windpipe.

twisted comb: A single comb where the points twist to one side or the other instead of being straight.

twisted tail: A condition where the tail lays to the left or right side and is not symmetrical with the body line; also called wry tail.

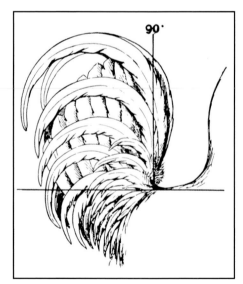

A squirrel tail is a tail that has more than a ninety-degree angle and is a defect. The exception is in the Japanese bantam breeds, where a squirrel tail is required. Do not breed birds with this trait, since it is genetically inherited. *Reprinted from the* American Standard of Perfection *with permission from the APA*

under color: The color of feathers or fluff under the first set of feathers.

vaccination: An injection of a dead microbe that stimulates the immune system against the microbe and prevents a disease.

variety: A breed subdivision that may be based on color, comb, or beard.

vent: The rear opening on the cloaca where manure is expelled and eggs are laid.

vulture hock: Found on feather-legged breeds where the feathers grow off the shank and touch the ground.

wattles: The pair of red or purplish flaps of skin that dangle under a chicken's chin.

worms: Internal parasites.

worming: The act of using special feed or medication to remove worms or their larvae from a bird's system; also called deworming.

wry tail: A tail that lays to the left or right side and is not symmetrical with the body line; also called twisted tail.

yolk: The portion of the egg used to provide the growing embryo with nutrients.

zoning laws: Laws regulating or restricting the use of land for a particular purpose, such as raising chickens.

This drawing clearly illustrates a wry tail. This is a deformity in which the tail grows decidedly to the left or the right rather than in a straight line with the chicken's body. This occurs equally in males and females and is a disqualification in all breeds and sexes. *Reprinted from the* American Standard of Perfection *with permission from the APA*

RESOURCES

Hatchery List by State

Commercial hatcheries and private breeders
will ship chicks directly to your home or a
nearby post office. Use this list to contact
them for a catalog or price list. Many also
handle hatching eggs and poultry supplies.
Some may only drop-ship chicks from
other sources.

Alabama
S&G Poultry, LLC
P.O. Box 2363
Clanton, AL 35046
(205) 280-3771
sales@sandgpoultry.com

Alaska
Sterling Meadows Hatchery
P.O. Box 744
Sterling, AK 99672
(907) 350-5558
info@sterlingmeadowshatchery.com
www.freewebs.com/
sterlingmeadowshatcheryalaska

Triple D Farm and Hatchery
5840 Gershmel Loop
Palmer, AK 99645
(907) 376-3338
www.alaskatripled.com

Arizona
Rockin' Rooster Ranch
Route 1, Box 214-M
Douglas, AZ 85607-9747
(520) 364-6654
dcaveny@primenet.com

Arkansas
Gabbard Farms
18213 Alpine Road
West Fork, AR 72774
(479) 761-2906
info@GabbardHatchingEggs.com

California
Belt Hatchery
7272 South West Avenue
Fresno, CA 93706
(559) 264-2090
orders@belthatchery.com
www.belthatchery.com

DarkEggs
P.O. Box 707
Pearblossom, CA 93553
(877) 572-8266
info@darkeggs.com
www.darkeggs.com

Southwest Hatchery
P.O. Box 1566
Blythe, CA 92226
(760) 921-2378

Colorado
Larry's Poultry Equipment and Hatchery
810 North Custer Street
Brush, CO 80723
(970) 768-1320
larryspoultry@bresnan.net
www.larryspoultry.com

Connecticut
Hall Brothers Hatchery
P.O. Box 1026
Norwich, CT 06360
(860) 886-2421

My Pet Chicken
501 Westport Avenue, Suite 311
Norwalk, CT 06851
(888) 460-1529
info@mypetchicken.com

Florida
Double R Discount Supply
3840 Minton Road
West Melbourne, FL 32904
Phone: 866-325-7779
sales@dblrsupply.com
www.dblrsupply.com

Gulf Coast Hatchery
4921 Rockaway Creek Road
McDavid, FL 32568
(850) 327-6364
sales@gulfcoasthatchery.com

Georgia
K & L Poultry Farm
772 Morris Road
Aragon, GA 30104
(706) 291-1977

Idaho
Dunlap Hatchery
P.O. Box 507
4703 East Cleveland Boulevard
Caldwell, ID 83606
(208) 459-9088
www.dunlaphatchery.net

Illinois
Nature's Hatchery
10413 South 248th Avenue
Naperville, IL 60564

(630) 428-7860
natureshatchery@yahoo.com
http://natureshatchery.homestead.com

Indiana
Shady Lane Poultry Farm
P.O. Box 612
Columbus, IN 47201
(812) 603-7722
info@shadylanepoultry.com
www.shadylanepoultry.com

Iowa
Decorah Hatchery
P.O. Box 205
406 West Water Street
Decorah, IA 52101
(800) 944-6503
decorahhatchery@oneota.net
www.decorahhatchery.com

Hoover's Hatchery, Inc.
P.O. Box 200
Rudd, IA 50471
(800) 247-7014
hoovers@omnitelcom.com
www.hoovershatchery.com

Murray McMurray Hatchery
P.O. Box 458
191 Closz Drive
Webster City, IA 50595
(800) 456-3280
www.mcmurrayhatchery.com

Sand Hill Preservation Center
1878 230th Street
Calamus, IA 52729
(563) 246-2299
sandhill@fbcom.net
www.sandhillpreservation.com

Schlecht Farm and Hatchery
9749 500th Avenue
Miles, IA 52064
(563) 682-7865
poultry@schlechthatchery.com
www.schlechthatchery.com

Sun Ray Chicks Hatchery
P.O. Box 300
Hazleton, IA 50641-0300
(319) 636-2244
eadegraw@trxinc.com
www.sunrayhatchery.com

Welp's Hatchery
P.O. Box 77
Bancroft, IA 50517
(800) 458-4473
bkollasch@welphatchery.com
www.welphatchery.com

Kentucky
Rice's Poultry Farm
1274 Hancock Road
Wickliffe, KY 42087
brice@brtc.net

Maine
CM Game Bird Farm & Hatchery
P.O. Box 626
Calais, ME 04619
(207) 433-0115
cmgfsales@bellsouth.net
www.game-birds.net

Shady Hollow Gamebirds
40 Pond Lane
Morrill, ME 04952
(774) 273-0370
info@shadyhollowfarm.com
www.shadyhollowfarm.com

Maryland
Whitmore Farm
10720 Dern Road
Emmitsburg, MD 21727
(301) 447-3611
info@whitmorefarm.com
www.whitmorefarm.com

Michigan
Townline Hatchery
P.O. Box 108
Zeeland, MI 49464
(616) 772-6514
info@townlinehatchery.com
www.townlinehatchery.com

Minnesota
Stromberg's Chicks and Gamebirds Unlimited
P.O. Box 400
Pine River, MN 56474
(800) 720-1134 or (218) 587-2222
stbchix@uslink.net
www.strombergschickens.com

Urch/Turnland Poultry
2142 NW 47 Avenue
Owatonna, MN 55060
(507) 451-6782

Missouri
Cackle Hatchery
P.O. Box 529
Lebanon, MO 65536
(417) 532-4581
cacklehatchery@cacklehatchery.com
www.cacklehatchery.com

Country Poultry, Estes Hatchery, Inc.
P.O. Box 5776
805 N. Meteor
Springfield, MO 65802
(800) 345-1420 or (417) 862-3593
cme@esteshatchery.com
www.esteshatchery.com

Crow Poultry & Supply Co.
P.O. Box 106
Windsor, MO 65360
(660) 647-2614

Heartland Hatchery
Rt. 1, Box 177A
Amsterdam, MO 64723
(660) 267-3679
jnieder@ckt.net
www.heartlandhatchery.com

Marti Poultry Farm
P.O. Box 27
Windsor, MO 65360
(660) 647-3157

Nebraska
Central Hatchery
55485 833 Road
Madison, NE 68748
(800) 272-2449 or (402) 454-2336
rjr10@uswest.net
www.centralhatchery.com

New Mexico
Privett Hatchery
P.O. Box 176
Portales, NM 88130
(800) 634-4390
privetth@yahoo.com
www.privetthatchery.com

North Carolina
Seven Oaks Game Farm
1823 Masonboro Sound Road
Wilmington, NC 28409-2672
(910) 791-5352
cmcallister1@ec.rr.com
www.poultrystuff.com

Shook Poultry
3177 Poultry Drive
Claremont, NC 28610
(828) 459-0571
shookpoultry@shookpoultry.net
www.shookpoultry.net

Twin Oaks Poultry Farm
P.O. Box 55
Shawboro, NC 27973
(252) 232-8733
sales@twinoakspoultryfarm.com
www.twinoakspoultryfarm.com

Ohio
Eagle Nest Poultry
P.O. Box 504
Osceola, OH 44860
(419) 562-1993
www.eaglenestpoultry.com

Healthy Chicks and More
3503 Crooked Tree Drive
Mason, OH 45040
(513) 238-5735
healthychicksandmore@gmail.com
www.healthychicksandmore.com

Meyer Hatchery
626 State Route 89
Polk, OH 44866
(888) 568-9755
info@meyerhatchery.com
www.meyerhatchery.com

Mt. Healthy Hatcheries
9839 Winton Road
Mt. Healthy, OH 45231
(800) 451-5603
info@mthealthy.com
www.mthealthy.com

Ridgeway Hatcheries
P.O. Box 306
LaRue, OH 43332
(800) 323-3825
ridgwayegg@aol.com
www.ridgwayhatchery.com

Stichler's Poultry Farm
1120 State Route 603
Greenwhich, OH 44837
(419) 565-3197
stichlers@zoominternet.net

Oklahoma
Country Hatchery
P.O. Box 747
Wewoka, OK 74884
(405) 257-1236
info@countryhatchery.net
www.countryhatchery.net

Southside Hatchery
12447 NS 3570
Seminole, OK 74868
(405) 382-1346
johnallison2589@sbcglobal.net

Oregon
Early Bird Game Farm & Hatchery
353 Sierra Way
Grants Pass, OR 97339
(541) 472-9539 or (541) 955-8527
earlybirds2@hotmail.com

Lazy 54 Farm
P.O. Box 429
Hubbard, OR 97032
(503) 981-7801
hatchery@earthlink.net
http://lazy54farm.com

Pennsylvania
Clearview Stock Farm & Hatchery
P.O. Box 399

Gratz, PA 17030
(717) 365-3234

Hoffman Hatchery, Inc.
P.O. Box 129
Gratz, PA 17030
(717) 365-3694
info@hoffmanhatchery.com
www.hoffmanhatchery.com

Moyer's Chicks, Inc.
266 East Paletown Road
Quakertown, PA 18951
(215) 536-3155
orders@moyerschicks.com
www.moyerschicks.com

Myers Poultry Farm
966 Ragers Hill Road
South Fork, PA 15956
(814) 539-7026
myerspf@juno.com

Noll's Poultry Farm
P.O. Box 14
Kleinfeltersville, PA 17039
(717) 949-3560

Reich Poultry Farms
1625 River Road
Marietta, PA 17547
(717) 426-3411

South Dakota
White Butte Hatchery
11705 White Butte Road
Shadehill, SD 57638
(605) 244-7492
b.w.wiechmann@sdplains.com

Texas
Ideal Poultry Breeding Farms, Inc.
P.O. Box 591
Cameron, TX 76520-0591

(254) 697-6677
chicken@hot1.net
www.ideal-poultry.com

Leon Valley Trading Co. Hatchery
1800 CR 479
Gorman, TX 76454
(254) 734-2973
wood@cctc.net
www.leonvalleytradingco.com

McCallum's Flock
117 Linda Lane
Texarkana, TX 75501
(903) 791-3843
jamielmccallum@mccallumsflock.com
www.mccallumsflock.com

Randall Burkey Company, Inc.
117 Industrial Drive
Boerne, TX 78006
(800) 531-1097
sales@randallburkey.com
www.randallburkey.com

X-Treme Gamebirds & Poultry
280 Lacy Drive
Elgin, TX 78621
(512) 281-4182
xtremegamebirds@austin.rr.com
www.xtremegamebirds.com

Washington
Harders Hatchery
624 North Cow Creek Road
Ritzville, WA 99169
(509) 659-1423

Phinney Hatchery, Inc.
1331 Dell Avenue
Walla Walla, WA 99362
(509) 525-2602

Wisconsin
Abendroth's Waterfowl Hatchery
WB697 Island Road
Waterloo, WI 53594
(920) 478-2053

Purely Poultry
P.O Box 1065
Oshkosh, WI 54903
(920) 359-0554
chicks@purelypoultry.com
purelypoultry.com

Sunnyside Inc.
P.O. Box 452
104 Beltline Drive
Beaver Dam, WI 53916
(920) 887-2122

Utgaard's Hatchery
P.O. Box 32
Star Prairie, WI 54026
(715) 248-3200

Chicken Breed Clubs and Associations

American Poultry Association
Dave Anderson
1947 Grand Avenue
Fillmore, CA 93015
(805) 524-4046
danderson@keygroupinc.com
www.amerpoultryassn.com/

Ameraucana Breeders Club
Michael Muenks, Secretary/Treasurer
33878 Hwy 87
California, MO 65018
(573) 796-3999
michael@bantamhill.com
www.ameraucana.org

American Australorp Breeders
278 County Road CNA
Champion, MI 49814
www.australorps.com

American Bantam Association
P.O. Box 127
Augusta, NJ 07822
(973) 383-8633
fancybntms@aol.com
www.bantamclub.com

American Brahma Club
Sandy Kavanaugh
216 Meadowbrook Road
Richmond, KY 40475
(859) 369-7244
henshaven@localnet.com
www.americanbrahmaclub.com

American Brown Leghorn Club
Dennis Pearce, Secretary/Treasurer
P.O. Box 602
Stanwood, WA 98292
ablc@the-coop.org

American Buttercup Club
Julie Cieslak, Secretary/Treasurer
7257 West 48 Road
Cadillac, MI 49601-9356
(231) 862-3671
americanbuttercupclub@yahoo.com
www.geocities.com/americanbuttercupclub

American Dutch Bantam Society
Kristi van Greunen, President
1910 Union Street
Alameda, CA 94501
Kristi@fynbosfarmpoultry.com
www.dutchbantamsocietyamerica.com

American Game Bantam Club
Mark Rosen, Secretary/Treasurer
59221 East Highway 50
Boone, CO 81025
(719) 947-3006
mfireback@aol.com
http://americangamebantamclub.spaces.live.com

American Langshan Club
Forest Beauford
Route 5 Box 75
Claremore, OK 74017
http://tech.groups.yahoo.com/group/
Langshans

American Silkie Bantam Club
Carina Moncrief
23754 Spenser Butte Drive
Gavilan Hills, CA 92570
(951) 801-8368
admin@americansilkiebantamclub.com
www.americansilkiebantamclub.com

American Sumatra Association
Christina Blanch
7701 North County Road 925 West
Yorktown, IN 47396
christina@sumatraassociation.com
http://sumatraassociation.com

American White Leghorn Club
Ted Schwabrow
334 Moonlawn Road
Troy, NY 12180

American Wyandotte Breeders Association
Stewart Jackson
6025 S Eaton Lake
Littleton, CO 80123
http://wyandottebreedersofamerica.com

Araucana Club of America
Fritz and Joyce Ludwig
207 Pickens Drive
Pendleton, SC 29670-9727
araucana@surfbest.net
www.araucana.net

Barnevelder Club of North America
Maggie Trussler
W8766 State Road 11
Delavan, WI 53115
meow@elknet.net

Bearded Belgian d'Anvers Club of America
Tim Bowles
312 O'Conner Road
Locasville, OH 45648
www.danverclub.blogspot.com

Belgian d'Uccle & Booted Bantam Club
3490 Pruss Hill Road
Pottstown, PA 19464
nniggel@verizon.net
www.belgianduccle.org

Chantecler Club of North America
Adrienne Blankenship
P.O. Box 43
Long Valley, NJ 07853

Cochins International
Jamie Matta
283 State Hwy 235

Harpursville, NY 13787
(607) 693-3433
mattsjt@aol.com
http://cochinsinternational.cochinsrule.com

Delaware Club of America
Christopher Fernandes
7403 Hidden Hollow Drive
Orlando, FL 32822
admin@delawareclub.org
www.delawareclub.org

Dominique Club of America
Bryan K. Oliver
943 West Bear Swamp Road
Walhalla, SC 29691
bryan_k_oliver@yahoo.com
www.feathersite.com/Poultry/CGD/Doms/
DCA/DomHomePage.htm

The Dorking Club of North America
Phillip Bartz
1269 Perbix Road
Chapin, IL 62628
(217) 243-9229
rooster688@hotmail.com

Faverolles Fanciers of America
Dick Boulanger
69 Perry Street
Douglas, MA 01516
(508) 476-2691
faverolles1@aol.com
www.faverollesfanciers.org

International Cornish Bantam Breeders
Association
Don and Dan Karasek
2504 State Road 133
Blue River, WI 53518
(608) 537-2734

Japanese Bantam Breeders Association
Terry Wible
5205 Guitner Road
Chambersburg, PA 17201
(717) 375-4573
http://home.roadrunner.com/~jbba/JBBA.
html

Marans of America Club
Brenda Little
3811 North 6th Street
Fort Smith, AR 72904
info@maransofamericaclub.com
www.maransofamericaclub.com

Marans Preservation Society
R. M. Presley
133 County Road 437
Athens, TN 37303
kdoctor1@earthlink.net

The Modern Game Bantam Club of America
Bonnie Sallee
P.O. Box 697
Pine Grove, CA 95665
(209) 296-8084
jbsallee@volcano.net
www.mgbca.org

Nankin Club of America
Mary Ann Harley
195 Macedonia Road North
Augusta, SC 29860
maryann4@bellsouth.net
www.nankinbantams.com

National Frizzle Club of America
Glenda Heywood
P.O. Box 1647
Easley, SC 29641
(864) 855-0140
frizzlebird@yahoo.com
http://web.archive.org/web/20030602183800/
www.webcom.com/777/nfcoa.html

National Jersey Giant Club
Robert Vaughn
28143 County Road 4
Pequot Lakes, MN 56472
(218) 562-4067
http://nationaljerseygiantclub.com

National Langshan Club
Jim Parker
3232 Schooler Road
Cridersville, OH 45806
polishman@watchtv.net

National Naked Neck Breeders Society
Ed Haworth, Secretary
Route 1, Box 322
Tahlequah, OK 74464

The New Hampshire Breeders Club of
America
Edgar K. Mongold
918 Stuckey Road
Washington Court House, OH 43160
(740) 333-5080
edgar@mongold1.com

North American Hamburg Society
Mary Hoyt
9365 North Santa Margarita Road
Atascadera, CA 93422

The North American Java Club
1408 Mason Bay Road
Jonesport, ME 04649
pamhlm@raccoon.com

North American Marans Club
Katherine Anderson
P.O. Box 1294
Goleta, CA 93116-1294
cari@netdoor.com

Old English Game Bantam Club of America
Sharon Garrison
316 Sullivan Road
Simpsonville, SC 29680
(864) 299-0901
syg4138@aol.com

Oriental Game Breeders Association
Eve Bundy
P.O. Box 100
Creston, CA 93432
(805) 237-1010

Plymouth Rock Fanciers of America
Robert Blosl
14390 South Boulevard
Silverhill, AL 36576
katz@gulftel.com
www.crohio.com/rockclub

Polish (Crested) Breeders Club
Jim Parker
3232 Schooler Road
Cridersville, OH 45806
polishman@woh.rr.com
www.polishbreedersclub.com

Rhode Island Red Club of America
Mike Hawkins
5963 Dwady Drive
Miami, AZ 85539
mhawkins43@hotmail.com
www.crohio.com/reds

Rosecomb Bantam Federation
Steven Beaty
P.O. Box 126
Portales, NM 88130
(575) 359-1074
firemannm@msn.com
www.rosecomb.com/federation

The Russian Orloff Club of America
Curtis Flannery

84505 500 West
Silver Lake, IN 46982
(574) 566-2426
flanfam@kconline.com
www.feathersite.com/Poultry/Clubs/Orloff/
OrlClub.html

Sebright Club of America
Mary Ann Bonds
P.O. Box 136
Ila, GA 30647
(706) 789-2869

Serama Club of America
Catherine Stasevich
9100 North 27th Street
Richland, MI 49083
seramaclubofamerica@gmail.com
http://seramaclubofamerica.webs.com/index.
htm

Serama Council of North America
Jerry Schexnayder
P.O. Box 159
Vacherie, LA 70090

Silver Wyandotte Club of America
Todd Kaehler
3534 Tuttle Road
Evansville, WI 53536

Sussex Club of America
sussex@geocities.com
http://geocities.com/heartland/ranch/2751/
sca.html

United Orpington Club
Don Chandler
201 English Mt. Road
Newport, TN 37821
doncharlott@bellsouth.net
www.unitedorpingtonclub.com

Wyandotte Bantam Club of America
Dan Karasek
P.O. Box 123
Fennimore, WI 53809

Wyandotte Breeders of America
David Lefeber, Secretary/Treasurer
8648 Irish Ridge Road
Cassville, WI 53806
dottestuff@yahoo.com
www.wyandottebreedersofamerica.com/
wbaindex.html

Mail Order Poultry Supplies

Bowles Poultry Supplies
312 O'Connor Road
Lucasville, OH 45648
(740) 372-3973

Charlie's Poultry Supplies
6346 Woodstock Tower Road
Fort Valley, VA 22652
(540) 933-6123

Clausing Company
P.O. Box 459
Nocatee, FL 34268
(863) 993-2542
clausing@desoto.net

Critter-Cages
305 North Harbor Blvd
San Pedro, CA 90731
(310) 832-9981
http://critter-cages.com

Cutler's Pheasant and Poultry Supply
1940 Old 51
Applegate, MI 48401
(810) 633-9450
cutlers@greatlakes.net
www.cutlersupply.com

Egg Boxes
P.O. Box 8651
Deerfield Beach, FL 33443
(800) 326-6667
www.eggboxes.com

Fleming Outdoors
5480 Highway 94
Ramer, AL 36069
(800) 624-4493
www.flemingoutdoors.com

Egganic Industries
3900 Milton Highway
Ringgold, VA 24586
(800) 783-6344
www.henspa.com

Ideal Poultry
P.O. Box 591
Cameron, TX 76520-0591
(254) 697-6677
chicken@hot1.net
www.ideal-poultry.com

Kemp's Koops Online Poultry Supplies
3560 West 18th Avenue
Eugene, OR 97402
info@poultrysupply.com
www.poultrysupply.com

My Pet Chicken
1253 Springfield Ave., Suite 163
New Providence, NJ 07974
(908) 464-3239
info@mypetchicken.com
www.mypetchicken.com

Poultryman's Supply Company
520 Agawam Road
Winchester, KY 40391
(859) 737-2636
info@poultrymansupply.com
www.poultrymansupply.com

Randall Burkey Company, Inc.
117 Industrial Drive
Boerne, TX 78006
(800) 531-1097
sales@randallburkey.com
www.randallburkey.com

Seven Oaks Game Farm
1823 Masonboro Sound Road
Wilmington, NC 28409
(910) 791-5352

cmcallister1@ec.rr.com
http://poultrystuff.com

Shop the Coop
(888) 290-1771
postmaster@shopthecoop.com
www.shopthecoop.com

Smith Poultry and Game Bird Supplies
14000 West 215th Street
Bucyrus, KS 66013
(913) 879-2587
smith@poultrysupplies.com
www.poultrysupplies.com

Other Organizations

American Livestock Breeds Conservancy
P.O. Box 477
Pittsboro, NC 27312
(919) 543-5704
www.albc-usa.org

APA-ABA Youth Program
Doris Robinson, National Director/
Coordinator
810 Sweetwater Road
Philadelphia, TN 37846
(865) 717-6270
nanamamabrahma@att.net

FFA
6060 FFA Drive
Indianapolis, IN 46282
(317) 802-6060
www.ffa.org

4-H
1400 Independence Ave. S.W. Stop 2225
Washington, D.C. 20250
(202) 720-2908
www.4husa.org

Books

American Standard of Perfection
The official breed standard for the poultry fancy in North America. Published by the American Poultry Association, the *Standard of Perfection* classifies and describes the standard physical appearance, coloring, and temperament for all recognized breeds of poultry.

How to Raise Poultry
By Christine Heinrichs
A comprehensive book that includes the history of poultry, essentials of keeping chickens, and information on the Society for the Preservation of Poultry Antiquities.

Raising Poultry the Modern Way
By Leonard S. Mercia
Covers unique feed formulas and hatching methods. Currently out of print, it is worth reading if you can find a copy.

Your Chickens: A Kid's Guide to Raising and Showing
By Gail Damerow
Covers basic aspects of chicken keeping. Aimed at a young audience.

Magazines

Backyard Poultry
145 Industrial Drive
Medford, WI 54451
(800) 551-5691
byp@tds.net
www.backyardpoultrymag.com
Published bi-monthly, aimed at the small-scale poultry keeper. Articles cover breed selection, housing, management, health, and nutrition, plus rare and historic breeds.

Newspapers

Poultry Press is a monthly publication in newspaper format that is essential for anyone who raises, shows, or has an interest in poultry. Includes articles designed to better your breeding, hatching, raising, and showing. Includes extensive classified and advertising sections to help you find all types of poultry, poultry supplies, show dates, and swap dates.

Poultry Press
P.O. Box 542
Connersville, IN 47331
(765) 827-0932
info@poultrypress.com
www.poultrypress.com

General Websites

www.backyardchickens.com
Originally designed for the urban backyard chicken owner, this site has information on how to raise, keep, and appreciate chickens.

www.the-coop.org
Provides resources and creates connections for small-flock owners raising, breeding, and showing poultry.

www.feathersite.com
An online resource for information about all domestic poultry. Extensive breed listing, breed photos, and chicken identification photos.

www.poultryconnection.com
Provides many links and resources for the poultry industry. The Poultry Forum and Poultry Promotion posting pages have daily action and reports.

University Websites

http://msucares.com/poultry/consumer/index.html
Mississippi State University Extension Service
Resource for the small-flock owner on reproduction and small-flock management.

www.ansi.okstate.edu/poultry
Oklahoma State University–Department of Animal Science
Lists chicken breeds with illustrations and extensive narrative detail.

http://poultryextension.psu.edu
Penn State Department of Poultry Science
Provides educational and support information for poultry flock keepers both large and small.

http://www.aragriculture.org/poultry/small_flock_information.htm#General%20Poultry%20Information
University of Arkansas
Use as a starting point to link to information about any problems your flock may be having.

http://edis.ifas.ufl.edu/pdffiles/ps/ps04400.pdf
University of Florida
Common poultry diseases listed.

INDEX

ABOUT THE AUTHOR

Tara Kindschi is an avid supporter of youth and the poultry hobby. Tara's work for these causes include acting as Sauk County's Poultry Superintendent, volunteering as a county-wide 4-H Poultry Project Leader and serving as Show Secretary for the Wisconsin International Poultry Club.

She is also an active member of the Badger Poultry Club. She has mixed a graphic design career with rural, agriculture-inspired projects whenever possible. She resides in Sauk County Wisconsin on a small-acreage, historic farm with her husband, son, and an array of animal species, including poultry, of course!